Parents for World Peace

Seven Simple Steps to World Peace

LAURA FOBLER

Published by
Union Square Publishing
301 E. 57th Street, 4th floor
New York, NY 10022
www.unionsquarepublishing.com

Copyright © 2017 by Laura Fobler

All rights reserved. No part of this book may be reproduced or transmitted in any form or by in any means, electronic or mechanical, including photocopying, recording, or by any information storage and retrieval system, without the written permission of the Publisher, except where permitted by law.

Some names and identifying details have been changed to protect the privacy of individuals.

Manufactured in the United States of America, or in the United Kingdom when distributed elsewhere.

Fobler, Laura
    Parents for World Peace: Seven Simple Steps to World Peace
    LCCN: 2017952730
    ISBN: 978-1-946928-10-8
    eBook: 978-1-946928-11-5

Cover design by: Alex McCarthy / www.book2cover.com
Editing by: Claudia Volkman
Interior design: Claudia Volkman
Photo credits: Emma Rottier

laurafobler.com

To my daughter, Emma,
without whom I would never have been
the woman that I am today.

I will never be able to express in words how grateful I am
for having you in my life—I will love you forever!

CONTENTS

Introduction 7
Chapter 1   The World of Today, Filled with Conflicts   15
Chapter 2   My Story   27
Chapter 3   An Overview of the Seven Steps   41
Chapter 4   Step One: Everybody Is Responsible for Their Own Needs   51
Chapter 5   Step Two: Always Refrain from Judging   61
Chapter 6   Step Three: Never Use Power   69
Chapter 7   Step Four: Be Yourself   75
Chapter 8   Step Five: Always Expect the Best Intentions   76
Chapter 9   Step Six: ME-Language   87
Chapter 10   Step Seven: YOU-Language   99
Chapter 11   Fitting the Pieces Together   109
Chapter 12   How to Stay Ahead of the Game   131
Chapter 13   FAQs   141
Conclusion   147
Resources   157

INTRODUCTION

"Darkness cannot drive out darkness: only light can do that. Hate cannot drive out hate: only love can do that."
MARTIN LUTHER KING JR.

FROM ALL THE remarkable moments I experienced in my life, varying from the day I graduated from high school, the day I received my master's degree to the day I got married, one day clearly stands out as the most extraordinary day I could ever have imagined: the day my daughter was born.

I experienced this particular period in my life as a roller coaster of emotions: starting in the wee small hours of the morning when I couldn't sleep anymore due to the increasing pain of the contractions and woke up my husband, who obviously wanted to join the party. Hours of intense discomfort and pain followed, as I gave birth the natural way, but I couldn't have cared less, as at the end of the day, the most beautiful, perfect, flawless human being was born: our daughter! The moment I first held her, all slippery and a bit purplish, I instantly fell in love with her. To me, this was the most beautiful, sweet, intelligent, and precious human being ever born! The days that followed were just as overwhelming as the moment our daughter had arrived into this world, and I loved every bit of it. I experienced a profound sense of love that I had never experienced before. This was a human being I wanted to watch over and care for at all times. A fiercely protective attitude emerged as the days went by. Even though I was never easily bothered by external sounds, I clearly remember how annoyed I was because I heard loud noises coming from machines that were repairing the roads outside. Those sounds could wake up my sleeping baby—were these construction workers mad? What were they thinking?

If you are a parent or a grandparent, and I assume you are, I'm pretty sure you can relate to my experience. It was only after I became a parent myself that I truly understood where parents in general are coming from. The pure and visceral love I felt for this small, brand-new bundle of joy was overwhelming—it was nothing like any other love I had ever felt before. I never expected to feel like this. I thought I knew how love felt, but this time, I almost behaved like a true lioness, as I wanted to protect my child from all evil influences. And I mean ALL evil influences. Even though global conflicts, gang-related issues, crimes, bullying people, and many other negative themes had never kept me awake, since they were not part of my daily life, I now felt extremely vulnerable. I was a grown woman who knew what the world was like. OK, that may be a bit exaggerated, but let's say that at my age, I knew how to get around most problems in life. I knew which neighborhoods to avoid and how to identify and respond to people with suspicious behavior. But now what to do? My newborn was so vulnerable! My daughter was still a blank slate in a world filled with people with ulterior motives, criminals, and many other people who could cause her harm instead of offering her a loving and benevolent environment. How on earth was I to protect her from all that? After being over the moon for a couple of weeks, now a feeling of anxiety and worry gained access to my system. I soon realized that our world has always been full of negative influences. Malicious influences would always be there, no matter what. No matter how hard our world leaders attempt to improve the situation, sooner or later a new malevolent energy would emerge and surprise the world.

I was pretty shocked by this realization. In the thousands of years that we have been recording our world's history, there has never been a moment of true world peace. This honestly had never crossed my mind in a way that scared me, but this time, it was different. After all, my child was not yet able to protect herself. She was completely dependent on others whom she trusted. People like me.

It is not my intention to scare anyone; nor am I a pessimistic person. Actually people who know me very well will tell you that I am always able to picture the sunny side. However, I'm not blind or stupid either. I'm very aware of the alarming nature of many conflicts; they are part of today's world.

Compared to thirty years ago, the world has changed a lot. I think the biggest change in our world has been caused by technological advancements. When the Internet became available, people interacted with other people they normally would never have interacted with. In this respect, the world has definitely become smaller, and there are so many benefits to this. Today there are many more opportunities than ever before to travel abroad and meet other people from all over the world and explore different cultures, both in person and online. And just think for a moment about the endless ways to stay in touch with them! When businesses began using the Internet, they found customers from all over the world with beneficial consequences.

However, unfortunately there are also downsides to this. When people have more interaction with others, there is also a risk of more conflict. After all, conflicts will never be completely eradicated, as conflicts arise when people interact; it's as simple as that. More interaction therefore means an increased risk of conflict.

Let me clarify it this way: When people interact, there are conflicts, period. When I want peace and quiet in the house because I'm writing a book while my husband is trying to entertain himself with loud music, we have a conflict! Conflicts like this are inevitable. They occur all the time, so I don't think eradicating all conflicts would ever be possible or even necessary. It's actually on the contrary! Conflicts provide a wonderful opportunity to deepen a relationship, provided one knows how to do it! In this book, I will disclose to you how to approach everyday conflicts so you will undoubtedly strengthen your relationships. On the other hand, the conflicts that scare me are the escalated, completely out of control, skyrocketed, sometimes even global conflicts. These are conflicts that cannot be undone easily. In general, conflicts have always been harassing our planet and its inhabitants. But the conflicts I'm concerned with are the ones that have spiraled out of control in such a way that hardly any citizen understands what originally ignited the conflict in the first place.

No matter how much I love the downsized world from today, the increasing and ever-emerging magnified conflicts petrify me! Especially because conflicts never totally disappear, despite the many attempts by our world leaders to solve them. One way or the other, they keep resurfacing in cold-blooded and merciless ways. And that is what worries me. How, when, and where will I or my child be faced with an attack? Who will be the next victims of terrorist actions? And how much damage do they leave behind? Our society has a curative approach when it comes to solving conflicts, reducing crime, and trying to force back therapy and youth healthcare, but shouldn't we take preventive action instead? This would not only save money and effort, but it would forestall a lot of trial and tribulation too!

Obviously, we need to take a different approach. We cannot change the world by imposing our rules on others. History indicates that world leaders have tried this method so many times before with wavering success. We cannot keep battling crime and investing more money in curative programs for victims. This way, we will always be overtaken by events. Instead, we need to raise children who don't display aggressive behavior in the first place, who don't even contemplate using violence or becoming involved in global conflicts. We need people who demonstrate empathy toward the needs of others. We need to change the world from the inside out. It is the only way our world can truly change for the better. If this is the case, how and where on earth do we start? The answer may surprise you, as the key may be closer than you think: in your very own home.

Wow! Can we really change the world starting in our very own homes? It may or may not surprise you, but yes, it is true. As long as you don't expect to see results overnight, this is the only way to a lasting change, as the world will change from the inside out through our children.

A young couple called David and Mary who participated in one of my parenting classes decided to learn the very same principles and skills that I will tell you about in this book. Mary chose to learn alternative ways to deal with her kids, because she did not want to punish their children. Instead she wanted to learn a more effective approach to parenting. She was fighting with her children on a daily basis and didn't know what to do anymore. David, on the other hand, was NOT very enthusiastic about learning these skills and the ideas, I can tell you! Nevertheless, he wanted to do Mary a favor, so despite very definite reservations, he agreed to follow the program. As they were moving along, practicing the skills and discussing them, Mary soon noticed a difference in the quality of their relationship. Shortly David discovered the very same thing. I had not known that they were actually on the verge of a breakup when they started the training.

I don't want to take credit for every positive thing that happened between them. However, when I spoke to them a couple of years after the program, David told me that the skills and ideas he had learned not only saved the relationship with his three children, which had been seriously damaged. The program also saved his relationship with his wife. Applying the skills completely changed David's life. Before the training, he had feelings of loneliness, shame, fear, anger, and desperation. He felt he and Mary were trapped in a downward spiral. Once he learned how to connect with his family, despite these negative feelings, he soon discovered the difference and he reported feelings of joy, love, and hope. As a couple, they weren't completely there yet. But they were definitely out of the danger zone and moving in a positive direction.

Now, I'm sure you think that achieving this level of success is only for others, but not for you—am I right? I'm sorry to say this, but you are so wrong! You can accomplish this too, as long as you take the time to learn how the system works and then keep practicing. You will be able to improve relationships with the people you love, the people who live close to you, the people you work with—in short, all people, including yourself! The journey will not be easy, but hey, you're not alone; I'm here to help! I have your back!

After going through my system, many people tell me that they never imagined that the seemingly slight changes in their attitude and their way of communicating would result in the huge changes they've seen in their lives. They've seen results they never even dreamed of. I'm convinced that once you start applying the principles and skills that I cover in this book, you will experience the very same thing. This book will change your whole perspective on people, on children, on yourself, on the world. Therefore, this book will change your life too!

In order to achieve this, I will tell you about the threats we face if we keep doing what we have been doing for thousands of years, and I'll explain how this has affected our world and how it will affect your child. Then I will cover five key principles on what to understand first and why you should adopt this view. Each section will be complemented by one or more exercises to make sure you not only fully comprehend the presented ideas, but can also apply them. After the five key principles, I will share the two skills all parents should master. These are also followed by exercises so you can start practicing them. I will also cover many real-life examples of how to put the pieces together, answer the most frequently asked questions, and give you practical guidelines so you will definitely stay ahead of the herd by using this system. After all, you want that change to start in your home, don't you?

Please bear in mind that this book is not intended to make you feel bad about yourself, your child, your parenting style, or anything else related to this topic. On the contrary, I know that parents try their best given the knowledge they have, whether that knowledge is helpful or not. I have yet to meet an ill-intended parent. It's not your fault that your environment may not have been very supportive, understanding, skillful, or knowledgeable! The simple fact that you're reading this book already makes me appreciate and applaud you, as you obviously want to take responsibility for the situation. In this book, I want to tell you things you may never have heard before, may never have thought about before, or never tried before. That is all fine—it's never too late! We are now here, and I want to help you raise awareness, so not only you and your child will benefit, but everybody around you and eventually the whole world too! You cannot change what you don't see or don't acknowledge, right? I hope it is now clear that I support instead of judge you!

Oh, one more thing: I think you will start to see things in a different light once you have read the entire book and understand the whole integrated system. So may I ask you to hold off making any judgment until you have read everything? I'm sure it will be challenging at times, but please, finish the book first and then decide how you feel. Fair enough? It will be well worth the wait, I promise!

Are you ready to take a deep dive into this topic and learn the Seven Simple Steps to World Peace?

I assume you are, so please get ready—here we go!

CHAPTER 1
THE WORLD OF TODAY, FILLED WITH CONFLICTS

*"If we are to reach real peace in the world,
we shall have to begin with the children."*
MAHATMA GANDHI

I OFTEN HEAR people say: "The world is one big mess; I don't know how one can ever resolve this chaos filled with conflict and war." I must admit that I don't pretend to have all the answers to our current world problems. On the other hand, I do see how we can all make our personal contribution to our world, so that in the end—that is, within the next generation—there is light at the end of the tunnel. We as parents need decisive insights so we don't have to rely on our world leaders to change our world. We have to change from the inside out so a ripple effect can take place and we can finally experience a world free of conflict. It is the exact same mechanism as how the world became the way it is now in the first place. Have you ever thought about this paradigm?

From my perspective, the world has been caught up in a vicious circle as far as inequality and, in particular, the use of power is concerned. After all, power is a widely used manifestation of inequality. Many countries, world leaders, groups, authoritarian people (teachers, managers, parents) use a power system in an effort to control people. Think of punishments, penalties, boycotts, (political) embargoes, sanctions, or discipline—the list goes on and on. Apart from the question as to whether these methods actually work (I will tell you more about these methods in chapter 6), using power on other people leads to negative feelings, because the "victim" has to defer to their own needs. Deferring to needs is simply inherent to a victim of power. After all, when one is forced to obey, one cannot take one's own needs into consideration.

The Power Loop

Take a child who has a need to relax and enjoy his new toy. However, his mother wants him to finish his daily chores first, and she uses power to get this done by threatening to take away the toy. The child loves the new toy, so he decides to defer to his own needs, leaving him with all sorts of negative feelings. When one's needs have not been fulfilled, it undoubtedly leads to negative feelings such as frustration, despair, or anger. It may come as no surprise to you that people who build up a lot of negative feelings (such as anger) have a high risk of becoming violent people! In other words, victims of power will often become power-using people themselves, thereby completing the vicious cycle. I call this the power loop.

Take a parent who wants to go home while their child still wants to play at the playground. The parent tells the child to stop playing and join them for the journey back home, because the parent still has some work to do. I think a scenario like this or very similar to this one has happened to all of us as parents, right? When the parent forces their child to go home, whether punishments are used or a reward is promised, either way, the child has to come home with the parent, thereby deferring their own need to play. This may lead to feelings of frustration or anger, simply because the need to play has not been met. Over time, when a parent keeps forcing their child to submit themselves to the needs of the parent, the child may become aggressive, leaving the parent in confusion. This is a child who used to obey and now is suddenly starting to rebel. Many parents then choose to become more strict—after all, the child wasn't responding well to their previous regime. Without realizing it, the parent and the child have become trapped in the power loop. I have personally seen this happen many times, but unfortunately becoming stricter does not solve the problems; it is actually quite the contrary.

Ignoring Children's Needs

There are many different ways parents don't take their children's needs into consideration, both consciously and unconsciously. Perhaps a parent cannot satisfy their child's needs to spend time together because the parent suffers from an illness. Or consider the single parent who has four children and cannot spend an hour a day with each child individually. However, in this book I want to focus on ignoring needs by using power, such as rewards and/or punishments; while using a power system is widely used by parents all over the world, this concerns a method in which needs are repeatedly ignored over a longer period of time. After all, the parent always gets their way!

Research has shown that children whose needs have not

been met over a long period of time are at risk of becoming psychologically damaged. Because children like this go through a variety of emotions while their needs remain unmet, they either become overly emotional people or start to build up an emotional wall while they eventually shut down their ability to experience feelings altogether. To a certain extent, they lose their ability to experience both their own feelings and other people's emotions too! When it has come to this, the situation has become quite dangerous, because in extreme cases, hurting or even killing other people would not move them at all. Would you be surprised if I told you that "world leaders" like Adolf Hitler, Joseph Stalin, Mao Zedong, and Saddam Hussein were all tortured as children? From this perspective, their victims were not the only ones who suffered from power abuse, as the perpetrators themselves apparently were victimized too. The same is true for bullies or terrorists. They too have often been victimized by others as children, thereby completing the vicious cycle.

It has been proven that all people have two sides to them: a loving, caring, and peaceful side and an aggressive, violent, and destructive side. Children who have been psychologically damaged by power are prone to becoming violent and destructive later in life (or become followers of a similar regime), while children who have been exposed to an empathetic environment as children choose to allow their peaceful side to blossom and will never be harmful to others! Wow! You may be wondering whether it is really this simple to protect our world from harmful, violent, and destructive influences. You may be surprised to hear that this is really true. Now you know why this subject makes me tick—why I'm so motivated to tell all parents that they should listen to what I have to say. The solution to world peace is in your hands. Don't wait for our world leaders, because if they were to ever find a solution to end world conflicts, the outcome would be put on us "top down," while adjusting our parenting strategies will make our children peaceful from the inside out, regardless of the actions of our world leaders. Isn't this amazing?

Luckily, not all victims of power abuse start using power themselves. In general, there are three ways in which people respond to power:

1. Fleeing
2. Fighting
3. Submitting

These three behaviors can be seen on all levels of our society and manifest in different ways. Most people have one dominant way of responding to the use of power, even though we all usually have different responses in different settings. I have personally exhibited all three behaviors in different situations in my life! It is important to state that all described behaviors can have other causes too. Not all people who quit their job or commit suicide are fleeing from power! However, when people do flee from power, they do this in a variety of ways.

1. Fleeing from Power. Some people try to flee from power so they will not become a victim again. Fleeing can emerge in different ways:

    a. *Literal escapes,* such as running away from home, quitting from a job, or relocating.

    b. *Psychological escapes,* such as abuse of narcotics and/or alcohol. Escaping in particular habits, such as excessive TV watching, excessive working, excessive reading, excessive listening to music, and so on also falls into this category.

c. *Lying.* Wow! Have you ever reflected on the idea that people who are lying could simply be trying to escape from power? Of course I'm not talking about white lies, but next time your child lies about having eaten a cookie, think about this for a second!

d. *Ultimate flight*: suicide.

2. Fighting Against Power. Some people simply will not give in to power abuse and will fight back. This can result in the following behaviors:

a. *Aggressive behavior.* As you may be aware by now, aggressive behavior evokes aggressive behavior in others, a clear example of an aggressive vicious cycle.

b. *Conspiring with siblings/peers against parents, friends, or communities.* An example of a generally accepted form of conspiracy is military treaties.

3. Submitting to Power. Some people submit to power for all kinds of reasons. Do not get blinded by the behavior alone, as complying often goes hand in hand with feelings of revenge and a deteriorated self-worth. There also is a risk of becoming a bootlicker. Finally, the suppressed feelings may eventually lead to an eruption of aggression.

As you can see, people respond to power in all kinds of ways, none of which are positive or beneficial. One way or the other, the boomerang comes back to us when we use power with our children, so we had better eradicate all power abuse from our planet!

Fortunately so, the world has already changed a lot over the last decades in many respects. If I take parenting of our children into consideration, there is one major change that cannot be denied: the growing interest in parenting and emotional health.

A Historical Overview

As far as views and beliefs concerning children and parenting, a lot has changed since thousands of years ago. People are becoming more and more understanding of children and the need for their emotional health. Unfortunately, this has not always been the case.

Thousands of years ago, many children were beaten, neglected, (sexually) abused, and even murdered. The Romans and ancient Greeks murdered and/or sexually abused many of their children, and these cultures were regarded as civilized, for crying out loud! After all, Plato and Aristotle lived there! During the Middle Ages in Europe, 15 to 50 percent of all babies were murdered and nobody mourned over them, because they were apparently unwanted. Infanticide went on until the nineteenth century, but don't disregard what is still going on today: in India, China, and Pakistan, babies are still killed because of a one-child policy or because female babies are unwanted. To tell you the truth, shivers are going down my spine as I'm writing this. The most shocking part to me is that children were not seen as people, but as a burden unless they could be useful, as work slaves or sex slaves. How can the needs of those godly creatures be ignored in the most horrific manner? However, I'm afraid there is much more.

Child sacrifices and mutilations have been regarded as normal for many ages all over the world because of certain cultural rituals or religious sacrifices. And the sexual abuse of children is still going on today in countries such as Thailand and the Philippines. Also, let's not start on what the Catholic Church has done to children when it comes to sexual abuse!

After infanticide had been abolished, people found a new way of discarding their children: abandoning them! Around 1750, the city of London was confronted with an astounding one hundred abandoned children per day ... can you imagine?

After abandoning children fell into disuse by the majority of people, children usually stayed at home; however, the parents used a very strict regime, requiring perfect obedience. Otherwise corporal punishments were used! Furthermore, children were still being used as work slaves and also secretly as sex slaves.

It took philosophers such as Jean-Jacques Rousseau during the eighteenth century to come up with the idea that children are not miniature grown-ups, but individual creatures with needs, wants, and feelings, and they should be treated accordingly. It wasn't until 1989 that the United Nations General Assembly passed the Convention on the Rights of the Child. Children are now recognized as independent beings with freedom of thought and speech. All members of the United Nations and some additional countries are parties to this treaty, with the exception of the United States of America.

To me, this short historical overview shows a lack of understanding about what children go through, both physically and emotionally, and the disturbing consequences of this hiatus in common knowledge. I'm so glad you, on the other hand, are willing to become educated, so I greatly encourage you to keep reading!

During the last couple of decades, interest in parenting and the emotional well-being of our children has been rapidly growing. In that respect, there is definitely hope for the future. However, there is still something quite huge that many parents tend to overlook.

Becoming Stricter

Even though many parents today are intelligent, well-intended people with an intention to bring up loving, caring, and peaceful children, too many parents think the best way to guide their children into adulthood is by using a power system! This is true even in The Netherlands, where I live and where children are supposedly the happiest children in the world. Here many people still think that when children do not behave according to their parents' wishes, the parents need to become stricter: using punishments when boundaries are crossed, such as removing benefits, or promising TV time or earning pocket money when children behave the way they are supposed to behave.

However, removing benefits or rewarding children with perks only leads to the power loop. Children who have been brought up like this are at risk of becoming violent, aggressive, or destructive people! Violent, aggressive, or destructive people are not the people I envision for the future of our world. How about you?

And while many so-called enlightened parents might not use a power system, they unfortunately do not realize that their parenting strategies promote inequality between parent and child, thereby also laying a foundation for hidden frustrations. It all comes down to using particular words and avoiding others. The adjustments that I promote in this book may seem to be minor, but I can attest that they have quite an impact on children and on our world! Whether you use a power system at the moment or not, I'm sure I will be able to enlighten you with knowledge and techniques that will help both you, your child, and your mutual relationship. Furthermore, in the end our world will benefit too!

I cannot stress enough how we cannot rely on our world leaders to solve this problem. This issue has to be solved from the inside out! It will not be surprising for you to hear that I raised my own daughter without the use of punishments or rewards. My daughter is so used to her needs being taken seriously that whenever she runs into inequality, which is inherent in a power system—for instance, in school—she's not afraid to open the discussion on this subject, often leaving teachers at a loss for words. In many cases, she apparently has been very convincing, as she has managed to turn situations around, leading to more equality, while many of her classmates who are used to a power system are very apprehensive to debate the whole subject!

This is what I mean by changing from the inside out. One can also see this inside-out process in groups of people, such as the Arab Spring, where people simply could not tolerate the system anymore and managed to destroy whole governments. Just imagine how our world would change if the new generation acted like this toward our current unjust systems! By now, I think it is clear that if we want to eradicate all escalated conflicts, we need an approach to parenting that shies away from all power and inequality and takes all parties' emotions and needs into consideration.

The New Approach

Considering the needs and emotions of all parties is exactly what I intend to teach you in this book, so please, for the sake of your children and our world, keep reading!

If parents keep using a power system in an effort to control their children's behavior or otherwise sustain inequality in their relationship, chances are they will be confronted with the negative consequences sooner or later.

In my search to provide you with the best information currently available, I re-read numerous books from my psychology education, I read countless new books, I went through an intensive course to become a Gordon Model instructor, I interviewed experienced instructors on this topic, and I tested everything myself. I first analyzed all materials and then identified the common denominators. It took me over a year of diligent work to come up with a simple system of seven steps. Not only did I test the seven steps on my own child, the countless participants of my parenting classes tested these techniques on their children over and over. I can now honestly say that implementing the seven steps I present to you in this book is the best possible action you can take to improve the current situation. Whether that situation is the situation in your home or the situation in our world, the result will speak for itself. If you want your child to become happy and thrive in this world, only focusing on their positive side and contributing to the world we're all a part of, you will have to accept your child for who they are, show empathy, and—last but not least—be yourself. This may sound cryptic or abstract to you, but throughout the seven steps in this book, I will tell you exactly what I mean and how you should implement the steps so your child will start transforming into the person they have always wanted to be! As a bonus, your child will become empathetic, assertive, and will never force their will upon others or pick up a gun. It may sound like a dream, but I can assure you, if you stick to the seven steps, you will get results that you never thought possible.

    I cannot wait to tell you more about the Seven Simple Steps to World Peace. Let's start our journey to our new world, free from conflicts.

CHAPTER 2
MY STORY

"It isn't enough to talk about peace. One must believe in it. And it isn't enough to believe in it. One must work at it."
ELEANOR ROOSEVELT

"NO!" I SCREAMED. "I cannot believe what I'm hearing; you've got to be kidding! Is this really true?" Eric was sitting in front of me. He was a tall, big man, in his late forties. Almost whispering, he was obviously feeling uncomfortable sharing his very personal experiences with me. The music in the little restaurant where we were sitting was loud, too loud, almost screaming in our ears. I was having a hard time taking all in that he just shared with me.

"Yes," Eric said. "Without a doubt in my mind. If it weren't for you, I would not be alive today, as I would have taken my own life."

I met Eric about a couple of years prior to that meeting. He had been my first official client. I had just finished my studies to be a career coach, and I was so happy with my new job! After finishing my master's degree in psychology, I began working in commercial roles, most of which were in a leading Dutch bank. I started out as a mortgage consultant, assisting clients in the complicated process of buying a house. After doing this job for a couple of years, I needed a new challenge and decided to further educate myself and become a financial planner. I worked with relatively rich people. I loved working with people, and I loved interacting with rich people as well, but I hated their quest for more money! I also was questioning my contribution to the world when I was helping rich people become even richer.

Therefore, I decided to pursue a managerial position, where I could focus on helping my employees. This way, I could turn away from demanding customers and see if I was able to support my employees in their personal and professional development. I loved the human focus of the job: the coaching, the motivational speeches, and brainstorming new possibilities to create a team spirit for my people. However, I disliked the paperwork and everything that had to do with numbers. I had to think of a way to get rid of all the boring tasks, and I was so lucky, as the universe had already decided this job wasn't meant to be. Only nine months after I started this job, I lost it due to economic circumstances. I became redundant, and I needed to find a new job. Soon I discovered my new path as an aspiring career coach!

It took me a couple of months before I landed my new job as a career consultant, almost as soon as I finished my studies. This was a job where I was able to put my newly learned skills into practice, and I was so ready to do that! I was presented with many, many great learning opportunities. One of them being my very first client, Eric. Eric was the kind of person you would not be able to overlook when he entered the room. At the same time, he was a very kind and social human being. He was a little bit shy, but once he got to know me, he soon started to pour out his heart. To be honest, this case was a little bit too complicated for a beginning coach like me, as Eric was experiencing difficulties in several areas of his life. First, he was having a conflict with his manager, which haunted him every minute of his working life. The conflict had escalated to a point where his boss didn't want to work with him anymore, so Eric needed to find a new job as soon as possible. He also had a rocky relationship with his wife, with whom he would eventually split up. To top it off, his two teenage sons were making his life difficult. He did all he knew to reach out to the boys, who ignored him altogether.

When I started working with him, I quickly realized that this was much more than merely assisting him to find a new job. After all, there were so many things going on in his life that needed to be resolved! Eric came to see me every week at 11:00 a.m. After our sessions, which lasted an hour, he always invited me to join him for lunch at a nearby restaurant. I was happily married and didn't want to send out a mixed signal, so I always politely declined his invitation and added that he was more than welcome to buy me lunch once he had secured a new job.

Weeks went by without any results. I started to feel frustrated. Eric still came to see me every week, but I didn't know how to help him any further. I already had tried everything I knew with him, but unfortunately nothing seemed to work. Then the time came to say our good-byes, as his boss didn't want to pay for any more sessions. To be honest I was glad to be put out of my misery! For years, I referred to my work with Eric as the least successful series of sessions I had ever done.

Fast-forward a couple of years. I received a phone call from a former colleague, who told me that Eric had finally landed a new job! I was very excited to hear this and tracked him down. First, I congratulated him with his new job, and then I reminded him that he had promised to treat me to lunch when he found a job. And that's when the conversation at the beginning of this chapter took place.

After we exchanged the initial pleasantries and after I heard everything about the new challenges in his career, I asked Eric how he looked back on the sequence of sessions that I took him through. To be honest, I had no idea how he felt about the period in which we saw each other every Friday. Little did I know, as his answer to my question blew me away.

He said: "I was going through a very tough time, and I was so grateful for our weekly appointments. I honestly don't know what I would have done without you. You were the only one in my life at that time who accepted me for who I was, supported me in what I aspired to do, and inspired me to get it done. If we hadn't had those weekly appointments, I would definitely have jumped in front of a train."

Wow. I needed some time to process all this. I thanked Eric for lunch, wished him the very best both personally and professionally, and left the restaurant. During the days and weeks that followed, I heard his words over and over again in my head. "If it weren't for you, I would have jumped in front of a train." Simply being kind, showing genuine interest, and using the right words could apparently prevent a person from committing suicide. This was amazing. This person was somebody's son. I thought of his parents, who were still alive and probably had no idea what was going on with their son. How would they have felt if they learned the truth? I was grateful that he allowed me to help him, even without consciously realizing that I was helping him. Apparently he had not received similar support from his parents, friends, or anyone else. At the same time, I felt sad. This person would seem perfectly fine to complete strangers. Yes, he was looking for another job, and yes, his relationships were a bit shaky, but otherwise, he was healthy, he had a nice house to live in, and he still had a more than average income. And yet this person was feeling so exceptionally unhappy that he had contemplated taking his own life. The most shocking part to me was that the simple act of being accepting, supportive, and inspiring was such a big deal to him that it actually prevented him from committing suicide.

Two years prior to this experience, I had attended a parents' meeting at my daughter's daycare center. It was the first time I met the instructor, who was very experienced and had three children herself. I had no idea this woman would become my master trainer when I signed up to become an instructor myself and later on, my friend and colleague too! The instructor explained how the Gordon Model should be used and elaborated on the principles behind the model. About thirty people attended the meeting, and most of them were very skeptical to say the least! They disagreed with most of what the instructor said, which made me feel quite uncomfortable. At the same time, however, I felt as if I had come home.

I could have put this model together myself, as all the beliefs and ideas behind it were somehow innate. The instructor mentioned the book *Parent Effectiveness Training: The Proven*

Program for Raising Responsible Children that Thomas Gordon had written, but it took me some time before I took the next step. A few weeks later, my husband was in the middle of a fight with our daughter and in desperation pleaded with me for help. I knew the time was right and so I bought the book for him. However, before he was able to take a look at the book, I decided to read the first page myself. Before I knew it, I had read the whole book and loved every word of it. This was my bible—this subject made me tick!

Without actually realizing it, at that point I had already mastered most of the skills that Thomas Gordon mentioned in his book. I now know this is very rare; I learned from leading many parents' classes that most parents first have to learn about the principles and required skills and then learn how to apply them, which usually takes quite some time and dedication. I guess I had a head start thanks to my experience and training as a coach. I was very aware of my own communication skills as well as the effects (both wanted and unwanted) that communication skills could have. And some of the communication skills Thomas Gordon mentioned came naturally to me.

This made me wonder if I should spend more time helping parents. Apparently most of the skills Thomas Gordon wrote about in his book came easy to me and seemed to work great—not only on clients like Eric, but also on my own child. Why couldn't I help others to do the same for their children?

The incident with Eric inspired me to think seriously about all this, but it took me a few years to finally enroll in an intensive course to become a licensed Gordon Model Instructor. I could not wait to receive my certificate, as I wanted to get started with parenting classes as soon as possible! I wanted all parents to know about this model and its wonderful skills, and it was my enthusiasm combined with my determination to teach the principles and skills that filled up my parenting groups with eager parents.

However, soon after I started the first group, I discovered that, while many parents thought the Gordon Model was absolutely fantastic, they perceived it as very difficult, often too difficult to apply. And it does take determination and a lot of willpower to master the skills. Over the years, I have seen only a very few parents able to use the Gordon skills effectively.

During the same period of time, as I taught the Gordon Model to parents, I read more books on this subject, including *Nonviolent Communication* by Marshall Rosenberg, *On Becoming a Person* by Carl Rogers, and many other books that aligned with this way of thinking. The more I read about these communication models and communication skills, the more it became clear to me that people who use these models, principles, and skills are nonviolent people. They aim to connect with others by actively searching for common needs and feelings, and they are accustomed to freely sharing their own needs and feelings. By doing this, they bypass violence altogether! I soon realized that this way of approaching others, whether they are children or adults, leads to a state of nonviolence. To take this even a step further: If parents approach their children with these principles and skills, it will automatically lead to a nonviolent generation! Children who are surrounded by people who apply these models will NEVER be aggressive!

Wow! Imagine this! A generation that is free of violence, free of conflicts, free of aggression, free of bullying . . . how would our world change if this were the case? Wouldn't that be amazing?

Once this idea came to me, I read every book I could find and attended all the programs that were aligned with this perspective—as well as programs based on views that I personally disliked. The idea of a conflict-free world fueled my activities. An adrenaline rush surged through my veins as I realized that this insight may be the very insight we needed in our world—an insight so very simple and yet so powerful. Because when parents get on board with this, the results will be well beyond everyone's imagination! I feel so excited for my child and my future grandchildren, as they may well enjoy a world that suffers less and less from conflict. I'm almost crying as I'm writing this. This is what I wish for everyone on this planet. Rich or poor, black or white, green or yellow—it doesn't matter. Everyone, and I mean EVERYONE, deserves a safe planet that is free from escalated conflict, terrorism, bullying, or wars. Aren't there enough challenges in our lives, such as health or career issues, without having to consider conflicts, terrorism, or wars?

The other thing I really love about this idea is that it is something WE as parents can actively contribute to our world. We don't need world leaders to do the negotiating or try to mend the broken bond. We as parents can actually do something extremely powerful to improve our world. Sooner or later, the world will become a better place. I prefer this to be sooner, though!

I gave up watching or reading the news a long time ago. Even if I were to assume that the news is unbiased (although I'm convinced it's not), watching or hearing it makes me feel scared, desperate, frustrated, and helpless. After all, there is nothing I can personally do about it. Now, I absolutely realize that our world problems will not be solved overnight after you have read this book and implemented its principles. I'm not that naive. However, if you read this book and implement the principles and skills that I explain, you will definitely see and experience results that you never thought possible, and you will become part of a ripple effect. Your child will definitely continue to carry the torch. I surely hope you will continue this journey, as your efforts will not be lost. They will slowly spread like an oil stain. Before you know it, your children's friends will be using the same principles and skills as I will teach you!

I was very happy to come across the book *Parenting for a Peaceful World* by Robin Grille. In this book, the author explicitly demonstrates with ample and profound research the connection between parenting based on power and violence in our current societies. The way a society parents has a direct connection to the amount of violence that society suffers from. Unhealed traumas caused by a parenting style which is based on power can lead to violent adults and thus to a violent society.

It is not my goal to redo all the investigation that Robin Grille has already done so thoroughly. The goal of my book is to be a manual full of practical solutions to problems you are facing today: how to handle back talk, how to set boundaries without your child feeling helpless or resentful, how to nurture empathy in your child, how to resolve problems so that all involved are happy, and so on.

The effect? More love, more harmony, more happiness, and much, much more peace. Not only will your home be at peace—our whole world will eventually benefit!

The solution I will present to you is simple yet effective, as I searched for a common denominator in all the books and models I came across that aligned with my perspective and stripped everything down to the bare essence. The ultimate solution is very easy to remember, and once you know how it works, it is impossible to forget! Even though the solution seems simple, it is not always as easy to apply the skills. Most people will have to practice to master the skills. But don't be afraid. Will you be able to learn them? Without a single doubt! Do the seven steps work? Absolutely!

As I told you before, I have never had any serious issues with my own daughter. While she has had many conflicts with her father, her grandmother, and her teachers (sometimes even several conflicts in one day), I think she can hardly recall any major conflict she has had with me. Only in very, very rare instances have we run into a conflict. (Hey, I'm human too!) Now, lest you think my daughter is a wuss, I can assure you that quite the opposite is true. Because of her, I am who I am today. I have worked with these steps over and over again, not only because I teach them, but also because I needed them desperately myself. There could not have been a more effective journey for me than to have a child like my daughter. I assure you: If you're able to deal with her, you can deal with almost any other child.

Therefore, I'm so proud and happy to see a confident, assertive, and very empathic young woman today, who takes care of her own needs and also takes others' needs into consideration.

But don't take my word for it. Many parents have used the very same principles and skills, and time after time, the results were AMAZING!

Take a woman called Mary. Mary was a kindergarten teacher who attended one of my courses. Mary wanted to learn how to approach children differently. Many kindergarten teachers use methods based on punishments and rewards in an effort to control children's behavior, but after years of using this method herself, Mary was searching for other solutions. First she learned the seven steps and started applying them with the children in her class. The results were simply unbelievable. She noticed that the children responded in ways that were completely new to her: They now solved their own little problems, such as when two kids both wanted to play with the same toy. They also started telling her about issues that were bothering them—worries about their friends or their parents, for instance. They had never done this before. Then she noticed the children becoming more and more friendly and empathic toward each other. This was astonishing to her, as the children were only three or four years of age!

But the most surprising shock was yet to come. Mary hadn't told anyone that she and her husband were on the verge of a divorce. This situation caused her so much stress that she had to take sick leaves regularly. Her colleagues were aware of her fragile physical condition, but they had no idea that this condition was the result of her emotional stress. After Mary learned the seven steps, she not only started to apply them with the children, but also with her own husband! Mary had a hard time accepting that her husband and she were growing apart, that a divorce seemed to be inevitable. However, once she started applying the seven steps, they both found a way back to each other and managed to prevent the dreaded divorce!

Or take Steven. I met Steven because his wife enrolled in a parenting class. A vast majority of the participants of the parenting classes are women, with an occasional man in between them. Usually the women coerce their husbands to join them, using blackmail or other ways of pressure. In this case, Steven's wife couldn't make him join her, but once his wife graduated from the class, she was now able to influence him instead of using some form of pressure. The next class, Steven enrolled. Steven was the manager of a large corporation. He was the kind of guy who made it clear through his body language that he didn't need any help as far as his work as a manager was concerned. Steven had seen everything, knew everything, and had a lot of experience that helped him cope with every possible situation. Or so he said! Nevertheless, Steven came to me because he didn't know how to handle his two small children.

As a manager, he was used to dealing with adults and knew how to get results from them. With his children, it was a completely different story. His children screamed whenever they wanted something. They never obeyed him. Much of the time they ignored him. They even SPIT at him when he told them to do things they didn't want to, such as cleaning up their toys. After the first couple of years in his parenting career, Steven was kind of desperate and didn't know what to do. Here he was, the big man who didn't need any help managing adults. Yet he was completely helpless as far as communicating with his children.

Soon after Steven started applying the seven steps, the way he viewed people changed. He started to understand why people in general behave the way they do and why his children were behaving the way they did. He started to listen and discovered a whole new way of communicating. As a manager, he had always used many "directives." He told people: "Do this!" and "Do that" and "Shut up!" He later discovered that, although his employees never liked his communication style, they did admire his professional skills and knowledge. Therefore, they coped with everything they didn't like about him. Steven started to implement the principles and the skills he had learned—not only at home, but also at work. The results, both at home AND at work, were AMAZING.

All of a sudden he now had the tools to connect with his employees, he knew how to stay connected despite an argument, and he was having a wonderful time interacting with his kids. His life changed completely. From a very mediocre manager, he now became a manager star. From a struggling dad, he now became a fabulous dad!

These are not isolated stories. People who keep practicing and therefore fine-tuning these principles and skills sooner or later get awesome results! There is no doubt in my mind that YOU will get awesome results too. The skills are simple and appear to be easy. For some people they are easy, while others will struggle with them for as long as they live. Whichever goes for you, you and your child will benefit from them! The process of learning and perfecting these seemingly easy skills will lead you toward a deeper connection with yourself, which in turn will also strengthen the relationship with your child. Mind you, this is not a trick or a program to teach you "some new skills." I have been experiencing this process myself as a rich, deep adventure, which resembles an inward spiral that never ceases to amaze me. I expect this process to continue for the rest of my life. I am grateful that each time I reach a deeper layer within myself, a new level of connection with both myself and my child is built. This outcome in itself is priceless to me.

Let's continue by taking a closer look at the seven steps,

because my guess is that by now you are more than ready to learn more about them!

CHAPTER 3
AN OVERVIEW OF THE SEVEN STEPS

"Peace cannot be kept by force;
it can only be achieved by understanding."
ALBERT EINSTEIN

AS WE HAVE seen in the previous chapters, the root cause of most conflicts in our world, whether they are conflicts inside our homes or conflicts outside of them, is the use or abuse of power. When a power system is used, the victim will respond in a way that will ultimately lead to a vicious cycle that will never end and usually leads to all sorts of traumas—the so-called power loop! If we want to break this cycle, we need to do something completely different. Thankfully, we can take responsibility and do not have to be victims in this. We can start an inside-out process so we will eventually be able to break the vicious cycle and start healing our world.

Traumas

Many people, perhaps most people, grow up with all kinds of traumas, both small and big ones. Many traumas originate from parents' inability to deal with negative emotions effectively, whether these negative emotions stem from the parents' own abuse of power or from any other negative experience that we all have to endure once in a while. After all, for generations, most people were simply not aware of the importance of emotions, let alone knew how to deal with them effectively. Therefore, they ignored emotions altogether.

Fortunately, not all people need professional therapy to heal traumas in order to function in a normal manner, and I hope my child will never need professional therapy either. Not because needing therapy is shameful, scandalous, or in any other way negative. On the contrary, I hope my child will never need therapy because of the ill-fated occasions precipitating the need for therapy! Think of lost jobs; unhappy or broken relationships; addictions, including alcohol or narcotics; the list goes on and on! Whichever perspective one chooses, therapy is always a curative process where one has experienced a trauma. A main goal in my parenting is to prevent as many traumas in my child as I possibly can, and I'm grateful that I now know how to do this. I cannot protect my child from negative experiences, such as the painful experience of being bullied or the upsetting experience of not being invited to a birthday party. However, I do know how to prevent traumas caused by experiences like this, and I'll share them with you so you can protect your child too!

It's no coincidence that the Seven Simple Steps to World

Peace are all connected to three crucial building blocks of therapy as described by Carl Rogers and like-minded others: acceptance, empathy, and genuineness:

1. **Acceptance** is the ability to see another person as exactly as they are and not try to make them into someone else. Acceptance is linked to steps two, three, and five of the Seven Simple Steps to World Peace.

2. **Empathy** is the ability to understand the other person's point of view—both content and emotions. Empathy is linked to steps one and seven of the Seven Simple Steps to World Peace.

3. **Genuineness** is the willingness to be yourself. Genuineness is linked to steps four and six of the Seven Simple Steps to World Peace.

Transformation

The three building blocks of therapy are crucial for a therapist to master; otherwise clients will not make any progress in their personal development. When a therapist integrates the three building blocks into their personality and therefore in the therapy, the client will ultimately start to think, *When someone can accept me for who I am and understands where I'm coming from, I am apparently a worthy person*, and the client will start accepting themselves. This results in an increased self-worth, and they start the transformation into their ideal person: the person who they have secretly always wanted to be, but weren't able to become due to a lack of confidence. Isn't this amazing?

Just imagine what a process like this could mean for your child. And for our world, if everyone used these techniques on their children.

Seven Simple Steps to World Peace

I researched and analyzed the works of Carl Rogers, Thomas Gordon, Marshall Rosenberg, Aletha Solter, Rollo May, Viktor Frankl, and many others. Besides the three building blocks of therapy, I found five common principles and two common skills they all seem to use—or seem to abide by—in their models and theories.

If you apply these five principles and skills in your communication, your child will benefit. It doesn't matter whether you want to help your child to heal an existing trauma or whether you want to prevent traumas altogether, these principles and skills will help you either way! All parents can help their children avoid traumas, heal from existing traumas, and support their children as they grow up as confident adults with great empathy as well as assertiveness. This already sounds almost too good to be true, right? But hold on, there's more: Children who are brought up like this will never pick up a gun or think of abusing power in order to resolve their conflicts. Can you picture a world filled with such people?

In this book, I will explain the principles and skills of the Seven Simple Steps to World Peace. I will offer you several exercises so you will be able to implement the steps as soon as possible and enjoy the results that you have been longing for.

Here's a brief overview of the Seven Steps to World Peace:

Step One: Everybody is responsible for their own needs (chapter 4). First, realize that people behave a certain way because they think this is the best way to fulfill their needs. You eat an apple because you're feeling hungry. Your child paints on the wall because they want to express their creativity. If we start looking at behavior like this, we will never see a naughty or sweet child anymore, and most importantly, we will hardly ever get angry again, because we now see that others have needs too, just as we have. Furthermore, we are all responsible for fulfilling our own needs. That means that our children should learn how to fulfill their own needs as soon as possible so they become independent individuals who won't act in any negative manner, but instead take action to meet their own needs. People whose needs are fulfilled will hardly ever act in a negative way. Looking at behavior like this makes for building bridges between people instead of polarizing them.

Step Two: Refrain from judging (chapter 5). We cannot stop this automatic process, and yet we should refrain from verbalizing our judgments, simply because we can never know all the relevant circumstances that made someone behave the way they did. People tend to build up anger when they are judged, either positively or negatively, while refraining from judgment and trying to understand others and their motives creates understanding and compassion between people.

Step Three: Never punish or reward (chapter 6). There are numerous disadvantages of using a power system. To name just one: People respond to power in three different ways: submitting, fighting, or fleeing. When people submit themselves to power, the atmosphere seems to stay peaceful, but in fact they are building up anger and resentment inside. Both fighting and fleeing are not very helpful either in creating a peaceful environment!

Step Four: Being consistent is impossible and unnecessary (chapter 7). If you only were to stick to your own rules all the time, you'll have no opportunity to show your true feelings, because your feelings usually influence your mood and your willingness to obey your own rules. You don't have to consistently agree with your partner either. If you're consistent all the time, you are in fact lying to your child! Instead, when you're communicating your true feelings (i.e., "I'm so tired today because I had a hard day at work"), your children will learn to be empathetic and will soon know how to take someone's needs into consideration. These qualities are essential as we strive for world peace!

Step Five: Trust that your child will want to show their best behavior (chapter 8). Even though all people have both negative and positive aspects, your silent expectations of your child will prove you right. Your silent expectations may pervade the words you're using and thus inspire others to show their best behavior. So instead of: "If you don't return the change from the grocery shop, you will repay me!" try saying: "I have no doubt in my mind that you will return the change."

Step Six: Use ME-language (chapter 9). Use ME-language to talk about yourself. Learn how to talk and speak about your own needs and feelings. Speaking about your own needs and feelings doesn't generate any ambiguity, as only you can know whether your feelings and/or your needs are true. This may sound easy, but be warned that most people find it difficult to apply!

Step Seven: Use YOU-language (chapter 10). Use YOU-language when you want to put another person's needs or feelings in the center of your attention. Learn how to listen to others in a way that they will continue to speak, so they will share of themselves with you. This way, you will be able to connect with your child! Again, this may sound easy, but most people do not naturally use YOU-language. Using it may become THE game changer in your home.

Common Obstacles and How to Overcome Them

Once I introduce parents to the seven steps I just mentioned, I often hear the same obstacles over and over. In this section, I'd like to share them with you. Please study them carefully so you will not get entangled in the same problems!

This is a very nice and respectable approach; however, I'm not sure if this program is right for me. Are you kidding me? I created this system exactly for parents like you! Parents who love their children to death, parents who want their children to become assertive and independent one day, parents who do not want (or no longer want) to base their parenting approach on fear (punishments) or dependency (rewards), parents who are willing to do something instead of just hoping for the best. Does this sound like you? Because I have helped many parents implement this system, I have no doubt in my mind that I'm able to help you too! One thing and one thing only is needed from you to determine whether you will succeed in implementing the seven steps, and that is dedication. So please keep reading—I have your back!

I'm not the person with the right amount of dedication! If you think you may not have the right amount of dedication, I have great news for you: I am here for you! I will provide you with inspiration, show you the techniques that really work, answer your questions before you're able to think of them, and give you a kick in the butt if you need one! Believe me when I say that I'm not the person with the most dedicated mind myself. However, once I experienced these techniques actually working in a way I never thought possible and the beliefs behind the steps began to become reality once I was getting results . . . oh boy . . . I didn't need much dedication anymore. My child was reason enough to keep doing this. There's no doubt in my mind that this will be the case for you too!

I don't see why I should start using this system. If you're not sure why you should start using this system, I have an exercise for you. Please answer the following questions:

1. What is the thing in my family that needs most attention?
2. Will improving the relationship with my child help this situation or hinder it?
3. Have I already done everything I know to make sure that

all the positive aspects of the relationship with my child will stay like they are forever?

4. Will further improving the relationship with my child contribute to maintaining the status quo or hinder it?

I hope you now see that you will always reap the benefits of improving the relationship with your child, whether the relationship needs some repair or you simply want to invest in the relationship so it will be less vulnerable to harmful influences. Either way, once you experience the results of this system, you will never want to go back to your old method!

I don't have a mentor. This is not true! You now have me! I'm here for you; I have your back, I promise! And I'm handy too—I have materialized into a book so you can pick me up and take me anywhere you're going. In this book, you will find answers to many of your questions. If you still have more questions, please don't hesitate to contact me; I would love to hear from you, and I promise to reply personally! Just shoot an email to info@laurafobler.com. I'm open 24/7!

I don't have the time! This obstacle may be the best obstacle of all; therefore, I saved it for last. Not having the time to learn this may actually be a blessing in disguise. Learning new things requires effort. But what if I told you that you could practice these skills on anyone in any given situation? If you're a salesperson, you can practice the skills on your clients. If you're a teacher, you can use them on your pupils. If you're a doctor, your patients will benefit from you. In short: If you're busy, you usually interact with many people, and all those people can serve as practice material. So the busier you are, the faster you will learn the skills!

Now, please strap on your seat belts, because we're about to embark on a fascinating journey. I can't wait to tell you everything you need to know!

CHAPTER 4
STEP ONE: EVERYBODY IS RESPONSIBLE FOR THEIR OWN NEEDS

*When we are no longer able to change a situation—
we are challenged to change ourselves.*
VIKTOR E. FRANKL

WHEN I SAY everybody is responsible for their own needs, I mean that you are responsible for your needs and your child is responsible for his or her needs. This may seem like an odd statement, but did you ever realize that needs are the reason why we behave in the first place?

People Want to Fulfill Their Needs

Parents sometimes ask me why their children are badgering and pestering them. When the parent asks their child to avoid certain behavior, such as screaming out loud when a family member is still sleeping or walking away in a busy supermarket, the child ignores the warnings time after time and does it anyway. Parents wonder: "Aren't my children supposed to be obedient?" and "Why don't they take other people into consideration?" Seemingly disobedient behavior like this usually gets parents steamed up.

My reply to these kind of matters is as follows: Children are not in this world to pester or conspire against their parents. Children are usually very loyal to their parents and hold them close to their hearts. There are very few children who do not want to see their parents happy and content. However, if this is the case, why on earth do children behave like this regardless of their parents' wishes?

Well, it all comes down to the following principle: **All behavior is driven by attempts to fulfill needs.** (Note: What I refer to as *needs*, others may call *drives*, *demands*, or *wants*.) When I'm feeling hungry, I go to the kitchen and grab something to eat. When I'm feeling sleepy, I go to bed to get some rest. When I'm in the mood for relaxation, I go out for a walk, watch a movie, or call a friend to catch up. As adults, it's usually easy to fulfill our own needs (food, sleep, relaxation), as we mostly make our own decisions and are aware of social restrictions.

For most children, however, this is not the case. They haven't learned everything they need to learn in order to function independently in our society. And yet the same principle is still true: All children behave the way they do because they too want to fulfill their needs. So back to the original question: Why do children scream out loud while their family members are still sleeping? Do they want to bully their parents? No, usually this is not the case. They may have a need to relax by discharging their excess energy. Or they may have the need to be heard—literally.

We All Have Needs

All humans have needs. This can be seen at infancy. Babies signal their needs through crying. They don't have any other way to reach out to their caregivers. When they have a need for food, they cry until someone feeds them. When they have a need for love, they cry until someone cuddles them. When they have a need for sleep, they cry until someone puts them to bed. With older children, it is pretty much the same. The difference is that they now have a larger array of behavior to use to express their needs. However, the principle is still the same: Their behavior is driven by needs. They hit another child because they have the need to play while the other child holds the toy. They nag their parents for new toys because they have the need for adventure. The common denominator in these examples is that the behavior one chooses is the behavior one thinks will satisfy one's need.

When I look at behavior this way, I instantly feel empathy. How can you hold a grudge against a child when they scratched their name into your car with a stone simply because they wanted to show you they could write their name but were oblivious of the consequences? This incident, by the way, actually happened: My sister wanted to show off her writing skills, and because my father understood where her behavior was coming from, he laughed his head off!

One time, my daughter, who was about six years old at the time, wanted to play with a friend who lived not far from our house. She was too young to go there on her own, so I took her there by car and then went to the supermarket to run some errands. When I returned home, I found my daughter and her friend in our kitchen. I was quite surprised to see them there, as she didn't have access to the key to our house. As it turned out, she managed to get into the house because she knew our neighbor kept a spare key and convinced her to unlock the door.

However, this was definitely not my main concern. As I opened the front door, I saw a flood of water coming from the kitchen and two smiling children standing on chairs behind the kitchen counter. *Oh my goodness . . . what happened here?* was the first thought that entered my mind. Before I had a chance to say anything, my daughter came up to me cheerfully, telling me that they had felt bored and decided to help someone. My daughter thought of helping me and then decided to go home and clean our two goldfish's bowl, as she knew how much I hated doing this. Fortunately, the bowl was not very big, but there still was a lot more water outside the bowl than inside it.

In this situation, I think many parents would get livid. After all, cleaning up the mess cost me at least one hour and took a lot more effort than cleaning the bowl myself. But in this case, because my daughter told me which need she was fulfilling, I loved her even more. This small human being wanted to help me the best way she knew how and was hoping to pleasantly surprise me! Well, she indeed succeeded in surprising me!

Each Person Is Responsible for Their Own Needs

In my parenting classes, the principle that everybody is responsible for their own needs is usually the first principle I discuss, and it often makes people frown! When I elaborate on this principle, I explain that when the participants feel thirsty, they should get themselves a drink. When they feel cold, they should bring up the subject of closing a window. When they feel hungry, they should eat something. When they don't understand something, they should ask for help. In other words: They should take care of themselves instead of expecting me to take care of them!

There are several reasons why I confront participants with this principle in this way. It all comes down to showing them how they could also treat their children as far as responsibility for needs are concerned.

Responsibility for Needs Greatly Reduces the Risk of Negative Behavior

When needs are not met, people experience negative feelings (such as hunger or frustration) and sometimes even show negative behavior (such as complaining or vandalizing). From my perspective, adults are people who take 100 percent responsibility for their own needs, but how can one take responsibility if one has lost the connection to one's own feelings and needs?

Only when one is conscious of one's own needs can one take responsibility to fulfill those needs, thereby reducing the risk of negative behavior. Unfortunately, many people in Western society have a hard time getting in touch with their own feelings and needs. I was no exception myself, but from my own personal experience and seeing this process in many participants, I can convincingly tell you that anyone can learn this!

I can now honestly say that with all the participants I've had in my classes, every single one soon started the journey of learning how to get in touch and take care of their own needs! If you start handing over the responsibility to your child, I'm sure you will have the same experience!

Responsibility Promotes Independence

We all want our children to become 100 percent responsible for themselves and become independent people. If we don't hand them the responsibility to fulfill their own needs, they will never learn how to get this done, and they will stay dependent on us forever. Being dependent on parents or anyone else for the long-term is not my definition of being grown-up. Now that I'm stating it like this, fulfilling our children's needs so children will have to hang around sounds quite selfish, doesn't it?

Handing Over Responsibility Is Relaxing

Parents soon realize that if they instill this principle at home, they will be freed from quite some care. Think of parents who are running around, busy collecting and washing their teen's sports clothes in time for a sports game while the teen lies on the couch watching TV, or parents who get up extra early in order to prepare breakfast for all their children while the children could easily do this themselves. Of course, there's an exception for children who are too small to take care of themselves or children who are unable to do this for whatever reason. However, for most of us parents, it's a relief to hand over the responsibility for another person's needs and enjoy the headspace.

You Cannot Know Other People's Needs Anyway

If getting in touch with one's own needs and/or feelings is difficult for so many people, including adults, you must agree that it is quite impossible for other people to know for sure which needs you may have at any given moment. I'm not talking about a situation where your needs may be obvious, such as entering a restaurant. The restaurant personnel may expect you to have a need for food! In general, I would not be able to guess anyone's needs just by simply looking at them. So if only you can know your needs and it's your own responsibility to fulfill them, you should take appropriate action, such as calling a friend, telling others what you need, or asking for assistance. After all, you are the only person who can know for certain what's going on inside of you! In chapter 9, I will tell you everything you need to know in order to make this happen.

Helping Others

Now that I've told you that everybody is responsible for satisfying their own needs, does this mean that you can't ever serve, indulge, or help others, including your own child? Of course not! I sure hope I'm helping you right now! If you want to help others, you can help them as often as you want, whether you do this in your spare time or professionally.

Think of hotels or restaurants where people wait on you to fulfill your needs. There are numerous occasions when we help others just for the sake of helping, because we have a need to help others and someone has a need for our kind of help. You might cook an extra meal for a sick neighbor. As long as you realize that you're helping others because you want to assist them, you'll have nothing to complain about. Otherwise, you simply hand over the responsibility to where it belongs!

It is paramount for you to understand that needs are the fundamentals of our behavior. When you start recognizing this, you will start to understand what's going on inside your child's mind.

Now that you know that your child is simply trying to fulfill their needs, does this mean that you ought to condone all behavior regardless? Fortunately not! In chapter 9, I will tell you which techniques you can use when you cannot accept certain behavior. For this first step, it is enough to understand that all behavior is driven by needs and that everyone is responsible for their own needs.

Exercises

Now that you know that all behavior is driven by needs, write down your own recent behaviors and think of the need you were trying to fulfill.

BEHAVIOR	NEED
Called a friend	Need to connect?
Purchased an ice-cream cone	
Slept on the couch	
Walked to the kitchen	

Now do the same with your child's recent behavior.

BEHAVIOR	NEED
Repeatedly asked for toys	
Teased their brother	
Watched a movie	
Made a mess of their room	

Note: Please remember there is only one person who can certify which need is involved and that is the person whose behavior you're assessing! Therefore, you can never be certain if you know someone else's need, but it will be very helpful to start thinking about needs, as this process will help you to get a better understanding of both yourself and those around you.

Are you fulfilling your child's needs? If this is the case, can you hand over the responsibility? In this exercise, using the chart on the following page, please write down some of your own behaviors and assess whether or not you are fulfilling other people's needs and also if you can hand over the responsibility.

My Behavior	Whose need is involved?	Can I hand it over?	If yes, how?
Make breakfast	My son's	yes	Let him do it himself
Returned my daughter's broken toy to the store	My daughter's	yes	Stand by her while she does the returning herself
Wash clothes	All of our needs	no	

If you need help doing these exercises, please don't hesitate to go to laurafobler.com/book for further assistance!

CHAPTER 5
STEP TWO: ALWAYS REFRAIN FROM JUDGING

*"When I look at the world I'm pessimistic,
but when I look at people I am optimistic."*
CARL ROGERS

BEFORE WE CONTINUE with what step two actually implies, let's elaborate on what a judgment in this particular context actually is:

> A judgment is your personal opinion or interpretation of a person or situation. Judgments can be both negative and positive.

You hear judgments all the time, and my guess is that you are using judgments all the time yourself:

"He is *late!*"
"She is very *intelligent.*"

"That child is very *naughty*."
"I cannot imagine having fun with those *dull* people."
"That's a very *good* question!"

Simple, everyday words like *kind, beautiful, ugly, indecisive, stupid, smart* . . . these are all judgmental words. I'm sure you can think of many other similar words yourself!

In this chapter, I will give you three reasons why you should eliminate all judgments from your language, as judgments can be harmful for both the relationship and the self-worth of the other person. Eliminating judgments from your language will not be easy—I have personally been there myself—but it is definitely doable, and the rewards will only encourage you to keep going!

Reason 1: It is impossible to know everything. Have you ever experienced someone telling you that you were late while you were under the impression that you were right on time? Did this spark a defense mechanism in you? How did this make you feel? Or have you ever been in a situation where a person had all sorts of judgments about you that you knew were untrue?

When I was a student, I was a member of the athletics team, and at some point in time, the team needed new members for the athletics board. I immediately applied. It wasn't only because I wanted to become more heavily involved in athletics; I also loved the idea of hearing things I would never have known otherwise. Somehow I have always had a hard time keeping up with the news, including the informal news such as rumors and gossip. Back then becoming a member of the board seemed to be a perfect way to meet my objectives. Besides the activities that came with being a member of the board, I also had to spend time on my psychology study. After all, this was the main purpose of being a student! Furthermore, I had a social life, in which having a boyfriend was an essential part.

One day we were having a meeting, and the president mentioned that help was needed for a fancy fair, where we wanted to recruit new members for the club. Now, I have family scattered all over the world, and hardly anyone in my family likes to travel or they simply don't travel for whatever reason. However, on this particular day, the day of the fancy fair, my favorite cousin from abroad was paying me a rare visit. My cousin was not capable of touring around herself, mainly due to the language barrier, so I accompanied her most of the time. Therefore, I was unable to assist at the fancy fair. In hindsight, I should have considered inviting my cousin to join me at the fancy fair, as this would have been a nice experience for her. At the time, though, that option never crossed my mind.

When I informed the other members of the board that I would be unable to help at the fancy fair, one of them started a monologue, without hearing me out first. When I think back on that whole situation, I find it pretty hilarious the way he was portraying his lack of communicative skills by not listening to me first. Instead he passed judgment on me in a very unpleasant manner. In front of the rest of the board, he declared that he personally knew many students who were merely interested in becoming a member of any committee or board for the sole purpose of beefing up their resumes. They were just interested in showing off their extensive experience on their resumes without ever wanting to do the work. People like that, as he put it, were "hollow people" from his perspective. He tried to use a civil way of expressing his ideas, by using the third person instead of addressing me directly, but in fact, everyone present at the meeting knew that he was talking about me!

I was completely stunned after hearing this. It was mind-blowing to hear someone pass judgments like those about me. He clearly wasn't interested in who I was or what my motives were. Also I was shocked that someone would think I was a hollow person only interested in building up my resume. It was so far from the truth that I wasn't able to say anything sensible at all. I managed to say something like, "This is absolutely not the case, but what do you know after all?"

This happened maybe twenty-five years ago, but what most sticks with me is the feeling of being invisible, of being unheard, and of the horrible feeling that I might need to share details I wasn't willing to share, simply because someone else was throwing around their judgments. Since then I've experienced numerous occasions where I was incorrectly judged, and each and every time it felt exactly the same as my previous experiences. Furthermore, each time I thought: *If you only knew everything that was going on, you would never judge me like this.*

And yet I must admit that to this day, I still have judgments about people. It's simply a natural process we humans somehow cannot repress. As a psychologist, I know this is a very normal and healthy habit, as judging people can protect us from harmful experiences. When a drifter approaches me, my antenna turns on immediately in an effort to judge whether I will be safe or not. However, verbalizing my judgments, especially towards my own child, is something completely different. I always try to make an intervention on my actions when it comes to judging others, especially when my own child is involved.

So the caveat is to refrain from judgments because one can never know the whole story! However, there are more reasons why you should keep your judgments to yourself.

Reason 2: Your child may lose their authenticity. Did you know that calling your child "sweet," "smart," "clever," and so on could actually harm him or her in the long run? Let me explain how this works.

When I hear parents call their children naughty or disrespectful, this always makes me chuckle, as children who hear this label often will think they are in fact naughty or disrespectful and will therefore continue to behave that way. In other words, parents who label their children in a certain manner reinforce the very same undesired behavior by doing so! When they use the label "naughty" or "disrespectful," while it's not great for the child, I think it is more harmful for the parent.

When parents label their child as being stupid or clumsy, this could be more harmful for the child, as these labels may cause the child to behave stupidly or clumsily on an ongoing basis, also leaving the child under the illusion that they ARE stupid or clumsy, which is very detrimental for their self-esteem.

You might be thinking: *Hey, I don't use those obvious negative labels. Instead, I use positive ones. Because when I use positive labels, my child will think they are beautiful, clever, sweet and will therefore carry on with this behavior, which is very much desired behavior.*

It is true that children continue with the behavior that is being reinforced to them through labels. However, have you ever thought about the authenticity of your child? Children may want to behave in a certain way but display other behavior—simply because it is reinforced in them.

In my own experience, people around me, my parents included, always called me "serious." Therefore, I thought I was serious and behaved seriously most of the time. I hardly ever smiled or laughed in front of strangers. After all, I was a serious person. May I remind you that phenomena like this usually remain on a subconscious level, which leads to the person involved, me in this case, not being able to change anything about it! I was well over thirty years of age before I realized that there was another side to me that I also owned: my humorous side. I hardly ever showed this side, because I was a serious person, but fortunately I can honestly say that those labels don't sound like me anymore! After hearing my story, my participants usually have no trouble sharing their own experience with labels. I've heard many mothers say that they were always the sweet child and had trouble being angry or assertive, simply because sweet girls do not behave angrily or assertively. Smart people had troubles displaying their weaknesses, because smart people supposedly can do everything.

Reason 3: Judgments reinforce polarization. I strongly believe that one of the major problems in our world is polarization. Polarization means that one way or another, a division is made into two sharply contrasting groups or sets of opinions or beliefs. It is a phenomenon that occurs on a daily basis and on all levels of our society. We simply want to distinguish the "bad" from the "good," the "young" from the "old," the "tall" from the "small," and the "kind" from the "cruel" in order to understand the world around us. It is human nature to judge people as soon as we meet them. Sometimes judgments are inevitable. Think of professionals who make professional judgments about people. Teachers in school determine which students score below average, mediocre, or best on tests. Organizations determine which of their employees are "high potentials." Doctors determine whether their patients are healthy or sick. Professionals have to make judgments in order to decide which further actions are most appropriate. Despite the fact that I understand why such judgments have to be made, it is still true that judgments contribute to polarization.

Long ago, I had a friend whom I considered to be a very close friend, even though I never verbalized her as my "close friend" or my "best friend" to anyone. However, on several occasions she spoke about another friend whom she called her "best friend." Even though I did not have a need to change the nature of our friendly relationship, the fact that I was obviously not her best friend stung me every time she said those words out loud. It also made me wonder who I was to her—her second-best friend? Her least-favorite friend? An ordinary friend? Did I matter to her at all? How would she refer to me when she spoke about me? It made me very uncomfortable. To this day, I still don't understand why a judgment like this should be made.

The same happens to me when I hear judgments about groups I'm not a part of. When foreign politicians call their country "the best country in the world," I often feel offended. Why is their country better than mine? I'm definitely not saying that my country is the best in the world, but from my perspective, every country has upsides and downsides, depending on one's personal needs. However, calling a country "the best country" leaves me feeling left out!

I'm not saying that judgments should be avoided at all costs: After all, teachers should know which students need more attention. I'm saying that we should be mindful about using (professional) labels and also not contribute to more polarization by verbalizing many other judgments.

Exercise
Now I'd like you to do a short exercise and answer the following questions:

1. Write down all the labels people have used with you in your lifetime.

2. Did these labels have any influence on your personality? If so, how did these labels influence you?

3. Which labels have you been using with your children?

Since you don't want to burden your child with labels that will eventually frustrate your child's efforts to develop their authenticity, I urge you: Please eradicate all judgmental words (including all labels) from your vocabulary. But relax, there's no reason to panic, because in chapter 9, we'll explore an alternative which is much more clear and more powerful than judgmental words could ever be!

CHAPTER 6
STEP THREE: NEVER USE POWER

"Peace comes from within. Do not seek it without."
GAUTAMA BUDDHA

OF ALL THE principles in this book, the principle in this chapter may be the most controversial as well as the most powerful one. So if you have checked out or are scanning through the book rather than studying the contents, I strongly urge you to check in again and pay close attention, as this chapter is a very crucial one!

First of all, let me tell you what I think using power actually means:

> One uses their power when one forces another person to behave in whatever way they want them to behave.

Forcing others to behave in a certain way can be done through two ways:

- through (threatening) punishments, including time-outs, withholding privileges, or blackmail

- through (promising) rewards, including bribing

Many parents live under the impression that rewards are a better alternative to punishments. Well, it is true that giving a reward may be a nicer thing to do than giving a punishment. The same is true when one is on the receiving end; receiving rewards is usually nicer than receiving punishments. However, either way the parent is always the one who gets what they want and the child is always forced to alter their behavior. If you look at it this way, this doesn't seem fair. One party always gets their way, while the other party is always forced to oblige.

If we want to raise children who care about others instead of only themselves, who are aware of other people's needs and emotions rather than being indifferent to others, who will talk in a civil manner about issues that bother them rather than resorting to violence, who not only think but also feel that we human beings are all equal instead of assuming that one side is always on the receiving end, who will never pick up a gun because they want to coerce other people's behavior, shouldn't we reconsider our own behavior first? If you also want all of this for your child, shouldn't you discontinue sending the implicit message through power systems that you always get your way while they don't?

If you have been using a power system on your child, I hope these statements are already enough for you to stop using it for the rest of your life. However, if you need more reasons, let's continue.

Fear and Dependency

Parents can only continue a power system when their personal power system revolves around two concepts: fear and dependency. After all, one can only execute punishments (or express threats/blackmail) when the child is afraid of the punishment. Otherwise the system will fail.

If I tell my child to pick up their clothes so I can wash them and my child refuses, I can say that in that case my child will not be allowed to watch their favorite TV show. If the child is afraid to miss the TV show, the child will probably pick up the clothes. In fact, the child will do almost anything I say simply because they are afraid for the punishment! However, if the child doesn't care about the TV show, or has other resources so they can watch the TV show whenever they want, I guarantee that this child will not be very likely to pick up the clothes. In this case, the power system will fail.

The same goes for rewards/bribes. The system can only survive as long as the child is dependent on the rewards. If you promise your child a candy bar when they have finished their homework, your child will only be susceptible for this reward when they really want the candy bar and have no other way of getting it. Otherwise, the system will fail.

Besides the reasons I already mentioned, there are many other reasons why you should reconsider using a system like this. They include:

- Your role in this system, as this system is quite complicated. You will need to adjust the amount of punishment and/or rewards to your child, depending on the circumstances. This takes quite some effort from you!
- If you continue to use a power system, your child will develop strategies to cope with it and will subconsciously choose between fighting, fleeing, and/or adjusting/submitting. Regardless of the coping strategy your child chooses, they will ultimately give up their authenticity. Think about it for a moment: Your child will ultimately give up their authenticity; is this what you want for your child?
- You risk that your child will model your behavior and start using their own power system on others—their siblings, their friends, or just anyone who does not oblige to their wishes. If we want true democracy for our world, based on equality and fairness, shouldn't we stop behaving like a dictator ourselves?
- When children obey, they do it because they fear punishment/blackmail, or they need the reward/bribe. They seldom obey simply because they're motivated to do so.
- The system usually works with simple behavior only (such as potty training), even though in many cases this doesn't work for potty training either. It is very difficult to teach children complex social behaviors (such as "how to share") using a power system.
- Punishing often leaves YOU feeling guilty, sad, desperate, unsuccessful, or filled with sorrow. This could lead to a variety of consequences—not the least of

which is you being unhappy as a parent and your relationship with your child being strained.
- Punishing or blackmailing your child will make them infuriated because they feel (and are) powerless and therefore feel patronized. Because many children want to show they still have some power and dignity left, chances are that they will rebel. Preferably towards you, of course.
- Sooner or later, you will realize that a power system is a very limited system, as your power declines as your child grows older. The older your child gets, the less fearful or dependent they normally become. Therefore, at some point your power will be gone. If you haven't learned to influence your child by then, you will be left empty-handed.
- Using a power system on children is detrimental for the relationship between parent and child, because children understandably despise feeling humiliated and powerless by their parents' behavior.

Exercise

If you still question the effects of using a power system, perhaps because most people seem to use it without hesitation, please answer the following questions:

1. Think of a situation in your life where somebody used their power to control you. Describe how this made you feel. How did you feel about the relationship with that person?
2. Think of a situation where you used power to control somebody else. Describe how this made you feel.

Isn't it incredible that usually both ends of the power spectrum feel negativity when power has been used? No wonder so many awful things could spring from this system.

Most parenting books and parenting experts encourage you to use a power system and let your child know who is the boss at all costs. I could not disagree with them more! From my perspective, a power system will ultimately keep our world the way it is now, filled with conflicts and wars, simply because we implicitly teach our children from an early age that using power is completely fine. No wonder they continue to use power as adults and think this is completely OK! If there were only one thing I could change about parenting styles throughout the world, I would definitely choose this one aspect! I hope that by now I have managed to convince you too.

CHAPTER 7
STEP FOUR: BE YOURSELF

*"Sometimes it falls upon a generation to be great.
You can be that generation."*

NELSON MANDELA

WHEN I CONDUCT parenting courses, the principle of "being yourself" is always part of the program. This principle stands for being authentic as a person instead of acting as the parent one thinks one ought to be. Being yourself means showing your true feelings and needs to your child. It's showing them that you don't know everything; it's sharing your insecurities with them and offering them your apologies when this is appropriate. Mind you: I don't mean that you should act like their friend and share everything that's going on with you, as not all information is appropriate for their ears. But if you allow your mutual feelings and needs to play a role in your decision making instead of letting the rules be overpowering at all times, you will feel much more relaxed and your child will have even more respect for you. They will see you as a person with qualities and insecurities who has merits and makes mistakes, just like any other human being. This will inspire your child to allow themselves to be human too and accepting of their own flaws. Also, if you communicate your needs and feelings, your child will learn that as humans, we are all connected by our mutual needs and feelings, as they have similar needs and feelings. Their needs and feelings may not be exactly the same as yours at any given moment, but your child will soon recognize that all people in our world have needs and feelings, which fuels their development of empathy.

What if you have a headache and therefore cannot allow your child to play indoors as they normally can? Simply tell your child that you have a headache and cannot tolerate any activities or noise at the moment. Your child might even offer you their special nurture! Are you elated about a new business deal and want to buy some extravagant gift for your child even though they just had their birthday? Why not share your excitement with your child and go for it? I'm sure your child will be elated too! Does decision making like this teach children something about boundaries? Or does it teach children that parents are people with feelings that can change at any moment? Many of the adults in my classes were astounded to hear that my four-year-old daughter asked me if I had finished my work, as she wanted to kick a ball against the outer wall of our house and knew I needed all of my focus to finish some challenging task first. Because she had heard me share my feelings and needs with her so many times, thereby showing her my human, authentic part, it was second nature to her to check in with me before she did anything.

When I tell my parent course participants about this principle, the individual responses vary, but the overall process of how participants swallow this principle is generally as follows: First they are surprised because they think consistency will lead to clear boundaries, then they are annoyed because they realize that they never heard this viewpoint before, and finally they feel relaxed because they understand that consistency takes a heavy toll on overall energy and they can now relax and simply be themselves!

When I first became a parent, I thought consistency was an important aspect of parenting too. Therefore, whenever my child hit our design table with the prongs of her fork, I told her not to do this, as it made small dents in our table. She continued this behavior, of course, and I (of course) continued telling her that she should stop hitting the table. This went on for quite some time until I got tired and couldn't do it anymore; I had no energy left to keep an eye on her. Still the behavior went on! I heard a voice in my head telling me to be consistent. Finally, I left the room or picked up a book, pretending to not see the unwanted behavior, as I simply couldn't bring myself to stay consistent. I know this is true for many other parents too because they've told me very similar stories. Some parents even pretend to fall asleep so they wouldn't need to stay consistent!

It is absolutely true that many parenting experts still urge parents to be consistent. But how is consistency possible when feelings and needs are subject to change? As far as I'm concerned, consistency is not only impossible, it is completely undesirable, because one way or another, if one chooses to stay consistent, one needs to hide one's true feelings. This way, children will never learn about feelings and needs and therefore will have a hard time evolving into empathic human beings.

Many parents are also worried that if they don't stay consistent, their child will become confused, because the rules appear to be flexible. Thought patterns like this imply that both rules and people are static, while I know for sure that my feelings change from time to time, depending on my mood, the setting, and the child I'm dealing with! If I were to stick to the rules at all times, I'd have to ignore my feelings, while my body will still send out its own signals through subtle body language such as tonality, voice pitch, posture, and so on. I'll tell you what really confuses children: saying one thing, while your body is saying something else! Most children are very sensitive creatures and able to pick up those subtle signs in your body language. By continuous "lying" (sticking to the rules at all times regardless your feelings), your child will first get confused and then ultimately lose their trust in their ability to pick up subtle signals. Are you willing to let this happen?

In a very similar manner, many people think two parents always need to take an undivided approach with their children. This means that when the two parents do not have similar feelings in a given situation, one of them would have to pretend! So let me reassure you: No, you do NOT always have to be on the same page with your partner!

When I realized that I didn't always have to agree with my husband, it felt as if a heavy weight had been lifted from my shoulders. My husband often expects me to be supportive and back him up. I never knew how to handle this, because while I was told that an undivided approach was beneficial,

I often disagreed with his solution! Today, it still happens that we disagree on trivial matters. It mostly happens when our daughter engages in behavior he finds annoying. When he pleads with me for help (because his own tactics aren't working), the response I give my daughter today is very true toward both the relationship with my husband and my own feelings. To me, this is an absolute win-win situation. In short, when it comes to consistency, I feel that a few basic rules in the house is a great idea, such as a rule for bedtime. If the rules are made with input from the children (unless they are still babies, of course), that would be absolutely ideal, as children tend to comply to rules much better when they've had a say in them. But in general, please don't get hung up on your own expectations of how to be a dad or a mom—just be yourself. Later in this book I will make suggestions on how to handle situations in which many other experts recommend consistent behavior on your part. I will also cover how you can support your partner while you're not on the same page. For now, I would like you to understand that consistency is simply impossible, unless you are a robot and have no feelings or needs of your own!

Exercise
Even though you do not have to be consistent, having some basic rules will make your life easier. Think of bedtime issues, how to handle homework, or how much candy will be eaten. Please be aware that:

- Rules work best if your child had a say in determining them.

- You should try to limit the amount of rules; think of ten rules at the most.

Which rules would you like to specify in your home?
1.
2.
3.
4.
5.
6.
7.
8.
9.
10.

Per rule, please describe if and/or how you could adjust the rule if this is appropriate.

1.
2.
3.
4.
5.
6.
7.
8.
9.
10.

CHAPTER 8
STEP FIVE: ALWAYS EXPECT THE BEST INTENTIONS

"There is a LIGHT in this world. A healing spirit more powerful than any darkness we may encounter. We sometime lose sight of this force when there is suffering, and too much pain. Then suddenly, the spirit will emerge through the lives of ordinary people who hear a call and answer in extraordinary ways."
RICHARD ATTENBOROUGH

I AM MORE or less fascinated by people and their personal perspective on the world. I love reading biographies, and I love watching TV shows in which human behavior plays a vital role. Every time I get an insight into people's thoughts or motives, one way or the other, my belief that judging is impossible is confirmed. Personally I am just as interested in hearing perspectives from so-called "good" people as I am in hearing perspectives from so-called "bad" people. However, I may be even more interested in "bad" people, as they never cease to intrigue me. Whenever I hear motives and personal stories from prosecuted and/or incarcerated people, a lot goes through my mind. For one, I often feel sorry for their personal background which is usually loaded with unfortunate circumstances, such as drug abuse, criminal behavior, a lack of education, and poverty. However, what strikes me the most every time I hear these personal reflections is the fact that many criminals persist in criminal activities because the people around them expect them to behave as criminals, and so they understandably don't see the point of trying to reverse their criminal behavior.

Wow! Can expectations of one's behavior really influence the behavior? Absolutely! There are several studies indicating how higher expectations of teachers influence their students' performances. This is called the "Rosenthal" or "Pygmalion" effect." The phenomenon that lower expectations lead to lower results is called the "Golem effect." You can read all about these effects on the Internet. Both principles are very closely connected to one of the reasons you should refrain from making both positive and negative judgments, as judgments may lead to situations where children will internalize their labels and start behaving accordingly, thereby giving up their authenticity.

Even though in chapter 5 I told you to refrain from negative and positive judging, in this chapter, I'm now telling you to always expect the best from your child. Isn't that contradictory?

Well, first of all, there's a huge difference between using positive labels and having a positive expectation of your child, as the latter should manifest itself in your attitude. There's a clear distinction between telling a child he's sweet, honest, and trustworthy and not specifically instructing your child to bring you the change after running an errand because you simply expect your child to return it. Do you now see what I mean?

Second, all people have a negative and a positive side to them. I sure have those two sides, our children have them, and I know you have them too. Depending on your expectations, your child will adjust their behavior accordingly and show their negative or positive side. Let me demonstrate how this happened to me.

Years ago, I was working as a freelance coach in a large organization. I had made an agreement with the manager that I could send them an invoice for the hours I had spent working for them. I had been doing this for over a year. I noticed that, because I had full responsibility to justify every hour, I could not help being more honest than I had even been in my life!

Whenever I was "chatting" with colleagues, I felt uncomfortable and would say, "I'm sorry, but I do have to get back to work. After all, this organization is paying me by the hour."

Both the manager and I were really happy about this agreement. The manager did not have to bother checking my monthly invoices. I took full responsibility in dedicating my time exclusively to work-related issues, and she fully relied on my integrity.

But unfortunately, things started changing, and not for the better. The manager found another position within the organization and left the department for which I was working. Another manager came along. Besides the fact that he was a male, he was older and had a totally different management style.

Suddenly, after I had worked for this organization for over a year, he wanted to check every invoice himself. I was fine with that. After all, I had nothing to hide. Quite the contrary! But at the same time, he started questioning my integrity by continuously asking me why I had to spend so many hours working on certain projects.

I soon realized that, to him, this was not a matter of learning new things. This guy was a complete control freak!

His approach was the same with everyone in the department. He questioned their integrity, wanted to know exactly what people were doing or planning to do, and continuously checked everything.

In other words: He did not trust anyone.

My reaction to his behavior may surprise you. I started to rebel. I started thinking, *If you don't trust me, why should I bother to be honest and responsible?*

And so, for every extra hour I worked, I sent an invoice. This was something I had never done before. I started to feel comfortable listening when my colleagues were recounting their holiday experiences while I was getting paid to work.

How does this story end?

At some point the organization needed to cut costs and therefore they had to terminate my contract as well. The manager didn't bother to thank me for everything I had done for them. He didn't even want to shake my hand. So after saying good-bye to him I stuck around for an extra thirty minutes to chat with my colleagues, sent him an invoice for my time, and bought my own farewell flowers.

In short, his micromanaging brought out the worst in me. At that time, I was really surprised that this behavior was part of me! ME, the honest, truthful, reliable person who behaved as such a short while ago?

How was this possible?

Later on, I learned exactly how this was possible. Because the first manager presumed the best of me, the very best of the best came out.

The second manager presumed the worst of me. He checked everything I did. I learned that I could not change his negative assumption, and therefore I started to prove him right as well.

Unfortunately for our society, the very same principle is true for criminals—they often even mention it themselves—as well as for our own children.

In the event that children are engaged in "negative" or even "criminal" behavior, do you now understand why becoming stricter typically doesn't work? A strict regime often derives from a place of distrust; otherwise those strict rules would not be needed.

A word of caution: if your child already has a history of past "bad" or even criminal behavior, please be mindful that these principles alone, especially this one, may not be the most effective approach to turn the situation around. In this unfortunate case you may want to turn to a professional for additional help. This fifth principle especially works best for children without considerable undesirable behavior in the past.

Exercise

Please sit down for a moment and ask yourself how you can show more faith in your child. Write down three ways and implement them as soon as possible.

CHAPTER 9
STEP SIX: ME-LANGUAGE

"One cannot reflect in streaming water. Only those who know internal peace can give it to others."
LAO TZU

IN THE PREVIOUS chapters, we covered all the necessary principles you need to understand before you can implement the necessary skills called ME-language and YOU-language. I applaud you for still being with me! Despite the fact that you need to know about the principles first, we are finally approaching the stage where you can actually implement the skills I'm telling you about. Once you start implementing these skills, you will soon know how they affect every single relationship that you currently have or will ever have: the relationship with your child, your spouse, your parents, your neighbors, your friends, your family—you name it, they will all benefit! Do not underestimate the effect that you will have on the people around you when you use these skills! Remember, when people feel heard, listened to, or are just simply content, they will not exhibit negative behavior such as aggression or violence. Just imagine how this ripple effect could affect our world, starting in your very own home!

Communication

Every communication process starts with a feeling or a need that the sender wants to share with someone else. The sender usually codes their feelings in some way. For example: A child feels hungry. The child codes their feelings by asking, "When is dinner ready?" or "Can I have some chocolate please?" or they may simply walk to the cupboard and grab something to eat. The person on the receiving end, usually the parent, should be able to correctly decode this message, otherwise the communication will be blurred.

Parents can interpret the message "When is dinner ready?" as the child being impatient, controlling, hungry, or curious. The most effective way to avoid all confusion would simply be to share the initial feeling, which was hunger. Therefore, if the child wants to convey their feeling of hunger, they could simply say, "I'm very hungry!" and then add, "When is dinner ready?" This way the parent is much better informed about where the question is coming from.

Have you ever told your child that they should put on a coat because it was cold? Did they protest, or did they obey immediately? I bet you had a discussion about the topic, with your child asking you why they should do this and you insisting that they should. Am I right? Unless you live in a hot region, of course, where the discussion may have been about wearing a hat!

Your dialogue probably went like this:

Step Six

> You: "Put on your coat!"
> Your child: "Why should I put on my coat?"
> You: "Because it's cold!"
> Your child: "No, it's not cold!"
> You: "Yes, it is cold. Now, put on your coat."
> Your child: "I am not putting on my coat; it's not cold!"

I'm not sure whether I want to know how discussions like this could end, but I can assure you that in many families, they can go on and on for a very long time!

Does this sound familiar?

In this particular case, the sender (the parent) gets themselves into trouble because they are not clear about who is feeling cold! I bet that the parent is the one who is feeling cold, not the child!

Many people, unaware of the benefits of separating ME-language and YOU-language, mix the two up.

I'll give you an example: When a parent wants to give their child a compliment, they might say:

> "You have been so sweet and wonderful. You are a fantastic child!"

With this compliment, I wonder: Whose sensations is this person really talking about?

Furthermore, what exactly is sweet, wonderful, or fantastic? Remember when we talked about judgments? So please, at all times, try to avoid words like that. If you keep using judgmental words, in most cases you're mixing up ME and YOU.

If I want to rephrase this sentence without any judgmental words, it could look like this:

"Thank you for reading your book without saying anything. Now I have been able to finish my work, and I feel so relieved!"

Do you notice how this message reflects the original sensation of the sender much better than the previous message?

Or instead of saying, "You have been a very naughty child!" try saying:

"My flowers have been flattened by your bike. Now I am very sad!"

When you use messages in which ME and YOU are mixed up, there are numerous disadvantages. The most important disadvantages are that they get YOU into trouble because you may end up with an endless discussion. Moreover, messages like this can influence your child's self-worth.

The caveat for effective communication is that you should always try to make a clear distinction between your own sensations and someone else's sensations. From there on, resolving issues will be so much easier, but most of all, there are so many benefits tied to communicating about one's own feelings or needs, most of which I will cover later in this chapter.

Using I or ME instead of YOU

When sharing your own feelings or needs, the first thing to be mindful of is that you should always use "I" or "me" in your sentence instead of "you." For example:

> "Once you get used to the neighborhood, you will like it!"

The sender probably means:

> "When I got used to the neighborhood, I started liking it!"

I honestly don't know why so many people use "you" when they mean "I" or "me." If you start listening for examples, you will hear or read abundant examples throughout the day, both in real life and in the media. For what it's worth, I will share with you my personal theory based on my personal experience: I believe that many people have shied away from their own feelings to such an extent that neither they nor the people around them even notice when they use the second person ("you") to refer to themselves. If you stop to think about it, it's really silly, isn't it?

ME-Language

As we discussed earlier, talking about one's own feelings, needs, or sensations is the most effective way to avoid any misunderstandings about the original feeling. After all, the feeling is the starting point from where the communication originates. This language is what I call "ME-language," as in all of these messages, everything I'm trying to get across is about ME.

How does ME-language sound? Here are a few examples:

"I feel wonderful after eating that salad!"
"I really love those cookies."
"I enjoy spending time with you."
"I read this book, and I learned a lot of new ideas and got many new insights."
"That really surprised me. I never expected that to happen!"

The Benefits of ME-Language

As I stated earlier, there are numerous benefits from using ME-language:

- ME-language is transparent and clear. There is no confusion about whose sensations are being mentioned.
- Others will show less resistance to my message. After all, my message is about me.
- Others feel more comfortable because I'm not judging them.
- It's hard to ignore ME-language. It appeals to the human, empathetic side of children.
- I don't have to play a role. I simply have to be "me."
- I get to know myself better. (I can honestly say that after using ME-language for quite some years, I still get surprised to discover my needs at times when I'm using ME-language. I then realize why I'm acting the way I do, because I'm forced into verbalizing my

needs, beliefs, or feelings instead of having them remain on a subconscious level.)
- My child gets to know me better. (I can tell you, your child WANTS to know you. Make no mistake about that. Children LOVE to see their parents for who they are, regardless of what they tell you. Also, this can be very helpful in the long run.)
- ME-language is congruent. My inner state matches my outer verbal message.
- Expressing my needs will make it easier to get help and support from those around me.
- ME-language is assertive; it's not passive or aggressive. I take responsibility for my own needs instead of playing the victim role.
- ME-language is an effective way to avoid misunderstanding and conflicts.
- ME-language helps to build trust and solidarity.
- My child will always be able to keep his or her dignity.
- The independence of my child is being encouraged. After all, it's up to my child if he or she wants to help—AND how he or she wants to help!
- ME-language is not detrimental to the parent-child relationship.
- ME-language does not contain a judgment. Therefore it accepts my child for who he or she is.
- My child will develop a positive self-image. (Remember that a self-image is developed by the things children hear from people around them. Self-image is not something the child was born with!)

Behavioral Description

In many cases, when you start expressing ME-language, you will want to add a behavioral description to clarify which specific behavior you're addressing. It is very important that your behavioral descriptions are neutral and do not contain any interpretations or judgments, as this may lead to a discussion in itself! For instance: "You always walk into the living room with your shoes on!" The word *always* may trigger an aggressive counter-response from the other person. "What do you mean, 'always'? I usually take my shoes off, but this time I left them on because I'm leaving the house in ten minutes—and you immediately accuse me of always leaving my shoes on?"

The definition of a *behavioral description* is: "A neutral description of what's perceptible of somebody's behavior in the here and now, without an interpretation or judgment." Here are some examples:

> "You walked into the living room with your shoes on."
> "You put on your coat."
> "You came home at 3:00 p.m."
> "You pointed at the tree."

Exercise

Now that we know what a behavioral description is, let's try to come up with some ourselves. This may sound easy, but I can assure you that most people need some practice before they can do this. Don't be discouraged if you need practice too. Even though "practice makes perfect," you don't have to be perfect at all! Showing your human, flawed side is just as ap-

Step Six

pealing to others and allows them to be human too, so never be afraid to just be yourself!

Change the following sentences from interpretations/judgments into behavioral descriptions. I already made a start for you!

INTERPRETATION/JUDGMENT	BEHAVIORAL DESCRIPTION
You are late.	You came home at 2:00 a.m.
You are lazy.	You've been sitting on the couch for two hours.
You are so sweet.	
You are so clumsy!	
You are a champ!	
You are so smart!	
You are so fast!	

Note: *There are several ways to do this; there isn't one specific way that is "right." If you would like to see some examples of behavioral descriptions, please go to laurafobler.com/book.*

Be mindful that if you give voice to your behavioral description and end up with a discussion about whether or not your description is true, you must have used a judgment or an interpretation, as it's almost impossible to have a discussion about a behavioral description. "You walked into the living room and took the remote control from the coffee table" is behavior that can be observed by you or even by strangers. "You wanted to confiscate the TV set" is an interpretation of that behavior, as there is no proof of the intention to confiscate the TV set.

The Rules of How to Create ME-Language

The rules of ME-language are fairly simple: At all times, talk about your own feelings or needs. If needed, you can add a behavioral description. Examples of ME-statements are:

"I feel so hungry; I haven't eaten all day!"

"I dislike the taste of spinach!"

"I'm so happy *you came to see me today (behavioral description)*; I've really missed you!"

"I love you!"

"When *you're jumping on the sofa (behavioral description)*, I feel worried. I don't have the money to buy a new one if the sofa breaks."

"I want to save the ginger cookies for the guests who are coming tonight."

When to Use ME-Language

Try to get used to your new basic language as fast as possible! ME-language is your first language for many statements, such as expressing your preferences or your likes and dislikes, but ME-language is also a great way to express intense feelings like excitement or anger. The more intense the emotion, the more appropriate using ME-language will be, as this language is filled with the benefits mentioned earlier.

Common Struggles and Mistakes

- Many people who start using ME-language sud-

Step Six

denly realize that they don't know themselves that well, and this interferes with their ability to form ME-statements. After all, one needs to be aware of one's feelings to verbalize them! I can definitely relate to this struggle. Sometimes I'm still challenged to express a ME-statement, simply because I need to switch off my head that cannot stop thinking and go back to my heart that can only feel. Once I do this, I then suddenly realize what I'm feeling. This process actually helps me get to know myself even better.

I'm quite confident that if you're struggling with this, you should continue to practice, as ME-statements will come out easier and easier as time goes on. Furthermore, not only will the people around you get to know you better, YOU will get to know yourself better too. What a great way to learn about one fascinating person, don't you agree? After many years of practice, ME-language now leaves my mouth without thinking at all!

- Except for the behavioral description, never mix up YOU and I/ME in one sentence. After all, ME-language is about me, remember? So saying "I need you to leave the room!" is not a ME-statement, as a true need does not involve a specific person. In this case, the ME-statement could be: "I need rest and I cannot have rest *when you play the piano (behavioral description)*."
- Some people think that all statements containing I or ME are ME-statements. Unfortunately, this is definitely not the case! "I think you are stupid!" is definitely not a ME-statement, because what does this say about ME?

A ME-statement could be: "I feel horrible; *you walked over my new garden plants (behavioral description)*."

Exercise

Remember the exercise to create behavioral descriptions? Let's take it one step further and add our feelings, so we can now make full ME-statements.

JUDGMENT	MY FEELINGS	ME-Statement
You are late.	Irritated	I'm irritated that you came home at 11:00 p.m. I have been waiting for fifteen minutes!
You are lazy.	Irritated, hurt	
You are so sweet.		
You are so clumsy!		
You are a champ!		
You are so smart!		
You are so fast!		
You are offensive.		

Note: *Again, there isn't only one correct feeling or one correct ME-statement. Many ME-statements are possible, depending on the feelings that are concerned. If you need help in your case or if you need inspiration for possible outcomes, please go to laurafobler.com/book for further assistance.*

Do you notice how expressing ME-language is much more powerful than judgmental adjectives could ever be? I hope you're just as excited as I am now that you know this, as in the next chapter, there's more to come!

CHAPTER 10
STEP SEVEN: YOU-LANGUAGE

*"Establishing lasting peace is the work of education;
all politics can do is keep us out of war."*
MARIA MONTESSORI

CONGRATULATIONS! YOU'VE MADE it to the final step! We're on the verge of putting all of the pieces together, so stick with me; we're almost there! Step six was about ME-language, and step seven is all about YOU-language. This second skill is the one that will help you to overcome communication obstacles. Once you understand how YOU-language works, you will never forget it, as the concept is so very simple! However, applying YOU-language may come more naturally to some people than others. In my experience as an instructor, I've learned that most people who struggle with this skill require a mental shift. They need to deflect their attention from their own perspective to somebody else's perspective—and let me tell you, I've seen a lot of people struggle to do this! On the other hand, struggling doesn't mean that they (or you!) won't be able to learn this! If you are really willing to learn this skill, there's no doubt in my mind that you will be able to learn it. I have seen many people succeed after a long struggle, so you had better not give up reading now!

Let's go back to the message from the previous chapter: A child asks, "When is dinner ready?" The parent could interpret this message as the child being impatient, controlling, hungry, or curious, to name several feelings.

Unfortunately, not many parents check their assumption first by asking, "Are you hungry?" Most parents ignore the initial feeling or need of the child and simply answer the question that is being asked: "In an hour!"

YOU-Language

In the case of a hungry child, usually there won't be a serious problem if you simply answer the question and ignore the child's initial feeling. But imagine a child that is being bullied in school. When the child and the parents drive to school, the child suddenly mentions, "I don't want to go to school." Imagine for a moment that the parent, consciously or unconsciously, ignores the horrible feelings of the child who is getting bullied and simply replies with: "That's too bad for you; you still must go." If you were the child, how would this make you feel? Would you feel encouraged to tell your parents what problems you're experiencing? Or would you rather stop talking altogether?

Most children choose to stop talking. I know I would if my feelings or experiences were neglected. It is moments like this where YOU-language comes in. Instead of ignoring the feeling that instigates the behavior, you now address the feeling by using YOU-language. You cannot always be sure which emotion your child is experiencing, so you have to guess! Don't worry if you guess wrong, as your child will immediately give you feedback. If you think your child is feeling bored at school and ask them: "You find school boring?" your child will say something like: "No, I'm not bored at all; it's the kids I hate!" Remember: YOU-language is all about the other person (YOU), never about ME, as that would be ME-language. At moments like this, where the emotions of your child are clearly present, YOU-language would be very appropriate to use.

The rationale behind YOU-language is that many people (and that includes children) are not aware of their own feelings, let alone comfortable sharing them freely. I believe this is due to our highly rational Western society, where emotions or emotional responses are often seen as "soft," "weak," "only for women," or "over the top." Regardless of the way some people may perceive emotions, this will not change the fact that everybody has emotions and people need to process their emotions properly in order to maintain emotional health. Most people are able to process their emotions properly when given the opportunity to talk about them.

If emotions are ignored, they stay inside our bodies, and sooner or later they will cause emotional and/or physical problems. In chapter 1, I covered what could happen if emotions are being ignored. By using YOU-language, you will help your child to become aware of their own emotions, help them to process the emotions properly, and eventually help them to restore the balance between emotions and rational thinking. This way your child will be able to resolve their own problems again and will not be inhibited by unprocessed emotions. Children who can resolve their own problems in a nonviolent manner is exactly what we want for our children and our world, isn't it?

Benefits of YOU-Language

There are many benefits using YOU-language. I think the biggest benefit is the implicit message you send to your child. By using YOU-language, the subject is all about your child, and you keep them in the center of your attention during your conversation. Who would not enjoy and benefit from undivided attention like this? I would like to encourage you to start listening to and analyzing everyday conversations. You will soon notice that most people will quickly talk about themselves when they hear a subject they can relate to. Therefore, emotions will not be processed effectively as the focus of the conversation suddenly shifts to the other person. From my perspective, using YOU-language with your child is a very valuable gift that heals almost any emotional wound. Some other specific benefits include:

- You don't judge; therefore your child feels accepted for who they are.
- Your child feels understood, because you name their feelings, beliefs, or needs.
- Your child feels comfortable, because you take the time for them alone.
- You understand your child much better now that you know their feelings, needs, or beliefs.
- You mutual relationship strengthens as you grow toward one another.

- Your child is able to solve their own problems because you helped them process their emotions by supporting them to restore the balance between emotions and rational thinking.
- Your child's needs and feelings are heard and understood. Therefore your child will become aware of other people's needs and feelings and will behave accordingly.

The Rules of How to Create YOU-Language

The rules of how to make YOU-language are fairly simple. However, the execution may not be as easy as you may have hoped for!

Name the feelings/emotions you think your child is experiencing. On top of this: never give your advice, opinion, or judgments!

This means that you should act like a verbal, emotional mirror: When you think you perceive sadness, you say, "Are you feeling sad?" When you think the emotion your child is experiencing is shame, you ask, "Are you feeling ashamed?" Again, you have to guess as to which emotions your child is experiencing, but sooner or later, I promise, you will get it right! Also, initially doing this may sound stupid or foolish. I can definitely relate to this thought, as I needed some time myself to get used to this way of responding. However, the more I used this language, the better my understanding of my child became, and the results were beyond my imagination.

Most parents are in touch with their children. They exchange information on a daily basis. My daughter and I, on the other hand, have a mutual attachment that is stronger than I could ever have imagined. I would say that we are inviolably connected. I don't underestimate the power of this language, as I strongly believe using YOU-language has played a significant part in achieving this. I am convinced that you and your child deserve this kind of a bond too, and I know beyond the shadow of a doubt that this is truly possible for you!

When to Use YOU-Language

YOU-language allows a two-way stream of communication, whereas ME-language is appropriate for a one-stream of communication—for example, to send a message from me to my child. YOU-language would be appropriate in the following situations:

- *To check our own assumptions.* When you hear "When is dinner ready?" you assume that your child is hungry, but you may be surprised to learn that they simply have a hectic schedule and need to reschedule their appointments.

- *Whenever you question what to say during a conversation, you can always rely on the power of YOU-Language to connect (or re-connect) with your child.* Most parents have to get used to the new languages and find themselves desperate for help in the middle of a conversation or even a conflict, as they are unsure what to say next. In cases like this, you can always use YOU-language and pick it up from there!

- *YOU-language is especially effective when you suspect that your child is experiencing intense emotions.* These emotions can be both positive and negative. If a child comes home from school jumping for joy and screams: "Mom, Dad, I got an A+ for my essay!" most parents would respond by saying: "That's really nice, darling—well done." Now that you've almost finished this book, I hope you will not say this anymore! To start with, you now have a much more effective alternative for judgments such as "nice" and "well done." Second, this is an excellent opportunity to respond using YOU-language! If your child is jumping for joy, an effective response would be something such as "You're elated!" Your child will probably affirm this by saying, "YES! I'm sooooo happy! It took me so much effort, and I never expected this!"

If you use YOU-language in situations where emotions are not very intense, you may find that your remarks will sound somewhat inane. If your child asks: "What book are you reading?" you are always free to ask: "You are curious?" or you could simply answer the question and name the title!

Common Struggles and Mistakes

- When I tell parents about YOU-language, they usually think it is unrealistic to use; they think it will take too much time. I agree that using YOU-language usually takes more time than instructing your children about what to do. However, the more you use

YOU-language, the more you will get to know your child, and this information will eventually lead to a situation where you will gain time instead of losing time. You first invest your time, then you will reap the benefits. However, if you're in a hurry, your child is in a hurry, or both of you are in a hurry, I agree, this is not the best time to use YOU-language!

- Children don't always want to talk, even if they are going through some intense emotions. They may even want to shut you out (temporarily) and go to their rooms with the door shut. Don't be offended when this happens—everybody needs alone time now and then, and this may be the case for your child, as painful and as hard as it may be for you. Believe me, I've been there, hearing my child cry in her room while I was completely powerless because she had shut me out completely. In cases like this, I highly recommend the use of nonverbal YOU-language. Respect their need for alone time and just let them know you're available if they need you. I can assure you, when they feel accepted by you, they will come back to you sooner or later!

- Parents who have never used YOU-language sometimes feel they are parroting their child's words. Child: "I don't want to go to school!" Parent: "You don't want to go to school?" Often the parent doesn't know what to say next. This happens when parents forget to focus on the emotions behind the words. In a case like this, try saying: "You don't en-

- *YOU-language is especially effective when you suspect that your child is experiencing intense emotions.* These emotions can be both positive and negative. If a child comes home from school jumping for joy and screams: "Mom, Dad, I got an A+ for my essay!" most parents would respond by saying: "That's really nice, darling—well done." Now that you've almost finished this book, I hope you will not say this anymore! To start with, you now have a much more effective alternative for judgments such as "nice" and "well done." Second, this is an excellent opportunity to respond using YOU-language! If your child is jumping for joy, an effective response would be something such as "You're elated!" Your child will probably affirm this by saying, "YES! I'm sooooo happy! It took me so much effort, and I never expected this!"

If you use YOU-language in situations where emotions are not very intense, you may find that your remarks will sound somewhat inane. If your child asks: "What book are you reading?" you are always free to ask: "You are curious?" or you could simply answer the question and name the title!

Common Struggles and Mistakes

- When I tell parents about YOU-language, they usually think it is unrealistic to use; they think it will take too much time. I agree that using YOU-language usually takes more time than instructing your children about what to do. However, the more you use

YOU-language, the more you will get to know your child, and this information will eventually lead to a situation where you will gain time instead of losing time. You first invest your time, then you will reap the benefits. However, if you're in a hurry, your child is in a hurry, or both of you are in a hurry, I agree, this is not the best time to use YOU-language!

- Children don't always want to talk, even if they are going through some intense emotions. They may even want to shut you out (temporarily) and go to their rooms with the door shut. Don't be offended when this happens—everybody needs alone time now and then, and this may be the case for your child, as painful and as hard as it may be for you. Believe me, I've been there, hearing my child cry in her room while I was completely powerless because she had shut me out completely. In cases like this, I highly recommend the use of nonverbal YOU-language. Respect their need for alone time and just let them know you're available if they need you. I can assure you, when they feel accepted by you, they will come back to you sooner or later!

- Parents who have never used YOU-language sometimes feel they are parroting their child's words. Child: "I don't want to go to school!" Parent: "You don't want to go to school?" Often the parent doesn't know what to say next. This happens when parents forget to focus on the emotions behind the words. In a case like this, try saying: "You don't enjoy school?" or "You're not excited about school?" or "You don't love learning new things?" It's trial and error, so try until you get the right emotion—your child will guide you along the way! You will know when you have found the correct emotion, as your child will very subtly change their tone of voice (usually a lower voice, but a higher pitch is also possible) and say something like: "YEAH!" It often looks like tension is released from their bodies; you see relaxation in their whole appearance. Some people also tend to sigh heavily once the tension is released. This is a very good sign! This may sound quirky, but if you try it, you will soon see what I mean. I think it is kind of special to witness this process!

- When emotions have been bottled up for some time and you succeed in naming the correct emotion, sometimes those emotions come out too fiercely, as when you lift the lid from a pan of boiling water. Don't be scared if this happens—it's a positive sign. After all, your child is releasing emotions! You will notice that soon after this happens, your child will start to calm down.

- If you feel you cannot accept your child for who they are, YOU-language will not be the most appropriate thing to use. If this is a temporary situation, for whatever reason, postpone your efforts and try later when you are able to accept your child. However, if this is a chronic situation, you may want to seek professional help for the benefit of both yourself and your child.

Exercise

Now that you understand YOU-language, let's practice creating YOU-statements! Try to name some possible feelings you suspect your child might be experiencing.

STATEMENT	POSSIBLE FEELINGS	YOU-Statement
The teacher is stupid.	Hatred, dislike	You hate your teacher?
Tomorrow is my birthday!	Excitement, anticipation	You're really excited about it, aren't you?
My dog died today.		
I don't want to swim!		
(Teenager says nothing and slams the door.)		
I'm on the football team!		
I'm too stupid to learn French.		
Nobody will come to my birthday party . . .		

Note: *There isn't just one correct feeling or one correct YOU-statement. Many YOU-statements are possible, depending on the feelings that are concerned. If you need help in your case or if you need inspiration for possible outcomes, visit laurafobler.com/book for further assistance.*

In the next chapter, we're going to put all the pieces together, so please stick with me—we're almost there!

CHAPTER 11
FITTING THE PIECES TOGETHER

"A mind at peace, a mind centered and not focused on harming others, is stronger than any physical force in the universe."
WAYNE DYER

IN THE PREVIOUS two chapters, you learned that you basically need only two skills to create the best possible relationship with your child. The first one is ME-language—our basic language—in which we speak about ourselves. We interpret everything from our own perspective. You've learned that ME- language is basically a sentence containing the word *I* or *me*.

ME-language tells your audience something about your needs, feelings, and perspective. You have seen how many benefits there are when you use language like this.

The second language is YOU-language. You use this language when you want to connect with your child. In cases when you want to resolve a conflict or want to reach out to your child and help them, you would use YOU-language.

Let me clarify the differences between ME-language and YOU-language:

- ME-language reflects my needs, my feelings, and my beliefs.

- YOU-language always reflects your child's needs, feelings, and beliefs.

- ME-language is our basic language. YOU-language is used only when we want to connect with others.

If you're in doubt what language to use, use YOU-language so you can secure the connection with your child.

Now that we know the basic differences, how do we know which situations call for which language?

The basic rule is: Use ME-language as your basic language, unless you want to connect with your child. Then switch to YOU-language. Switching from one language to the other is possible within a conversation. Just be careful not to mix the two languages in one sentence.

Let's have a look at specific situations and see how these two languages are effective.

Case # 1. My five-year-old and I are in the park. We have been playing for a while. After some time I would really like to go home; I've had enough of it. So I start expressing my feelings and/or my needs using ME-language.

"We've been here for a couple of hours, and now I really want to go home to do something else. The park is starting to bore me, and I'm hungry and thirsty as well." (I am using ME-language.)

My child responds this way:

"Well, I'm sorry that you are feeling bored. I'm not bored at all, and I'd like to stay for a while. I don't want to go home yet. I'm not hungry or thirsty." (My child is using ME-language as well.)

Now what to do? In this case, my child seems unable to listen to my needs. This is the case when HER OWN needs take precedence. So, now I want to connect to my child, because I want to know what is making her so enthusiastic about the park. I want to know more about my child's world. Also, since my child is clearly not responding to my request, I need to find out what is going on with her. So now I switch to YOU-language, and I try to reflect my child's feelings or needs by saying:

"You are still enjoying the park?"

Notice that I'm asking a question because I want to check whether I'm right or not. Saying this allows me to stay connected with my child, regardless whether I've guessed my child's feelings correctly or not. And my child will probably say:

"Yes! I just LOVE the park! I LOVE watching those people wandering around here. I could stay here all year!"

I now know what's making my child hesitant to leave the park and come home with me. Now I continue in ME-language to make my point. After all, I am still bored, hungry, and thirsty!

> "You really love watching those people; I can see how excited this makes you feel *(YOU-language)*, but I am BORED to death *(ME-language)*. I really don't know what to do anymore *(ME-language)*. I'm just sitting here doing nothing, and I have so many things to do at home *(ME-language)*. I get nervous simply by thinking about it *(ME-language)*. On top of that, I really want to eat and drink something now *(ME-language)*."

Chances are, that from this point on, my child will start feeling considerate and the two of us will be able to work something out, such as staying for another ten minutes and then going home. I have done this numerous times with my child from the time she was able to understand what I was saying. I never had any problems with her. Because I was considerate of her needs and feelings, she became more and more considerate of mine.

Case #2. I want to clean my home because I'm expecting guests. My child, who is sixteen years old, is at home reading a book. Since ME-language is the basic language, I start by expressing my needs.

> "I really want to clean our home. I'm also in a hurry because there are only twenty minutes left before I expect my guests to arrive." *(ME-language)*

Notice that I don't demand help from my child. I simply express my needs and feelings and hope for the best!

In some cases, my child may want to help me. In other cases, he may not. It is NOT up to me!

If you experience this type of situation, you may like helpfulness or hope for help. But it is up to the child. If your child feels considerate, he will probably help you out. If your child needs to study for an exam, he will probably not help you out.

Either way, when your child doesn't respond the way you were hoping for, try switching to YOU-language and see what happens. You could say:

"You don't feel like helping me out?"

Then your child answers:

"No, I really want to finish this thrilling book." In this case, the child thinks their need is more important than my need. That's fine with me, as this is not a matter of life or death. In other cases, things may be reversed.

In case you expect your child to obey you no matter what, I'd like to remind you of the disadvantages of a child who obeys all the time. Children like this will obey their peers as well and may begin taking drugs!

Case #3. My child comes home from school, goes to his room, and shuts the door. I hear him crying. Even though ME-language is the basic language, in this case, connecting to my child is more important. I'd like to offer to help my son, so I

start using YOU-language. I go to his room, knock on his door, and say:

"Honey, you seem really sad."

Notice that I simply reflect the apparent emotion. The rest is up to him. If he wants to talk, he'll let me in. If not, he'll ignore me or send me away.

Either way, I respect his wishes. It's up to my child to decide who is helpful and in what way. I don't show disappointment, sadness, or anger. My child has enough dealing with his own emotions. My emotions are too much. Also, I don't judge his manners by saying something like: "Don't be disrespectful!" This will only broaden the gap between us. On top of that, it will not help. My child has enough on his mind. If he behaves in a way that I cannot allow, for the sake of my child, I postpose my comments (in ME-language, of course) until my child is willing to listen to me again.

If he decides to let me in, I simply keep reflecting his emotions until he asks for advice; he will let me know when he's ready. Again, I don't get disappointed or sad when my child does not ask for my help. I am proud of my child who wants to deal with his own problems and solve them all by himself. I trust his ability to solve his own problems. I'm simply available in case he needs my advice after all.

Case #4. When I need to go to work, my child, who is five years old, starts to act angrily. I don't have a clue as to why she's behaving that way. Since ME-language is the basic language, I start expressing my needs with ME-language. I say: "I need to go to work, because I want to be on time."

Then, suddenly my daughter starts to cry. Now what do I do? I don't know what's going on. So I switch to YOU-language.

"You feel sad that I'm leaving for work?"

My daughter begins to cry even louder. (This happens sometimes when you hit the bull's eye. The emotion seems to explode, as if you've taken the lid off a pot of boiling water. Don't think you've done something wrong when this happens! In fact, it's a good sign! You've guessed the right emotion, and this allows for the release in tension in your child before she's able to be rational again and listen to what you have to say.)

Now, if I'm in a hurry to get to work, there isn't much I can do at this point, is there?

In this case, I use ME-language to say:

"I really want to talk this over with you, darling, but at this moment, I don't have the time. I promise to get back to you when I return from work this evening."

Don't be afraid to sometimes give preference to your own needs. That is what life is about. When you use YOU-language as well during your interaction, your child will feel more understood than if you don't use any YOU-language. When you're using both ME- and YOU-language during an interaction, remember to separate the languages. In other words: Never mix YOU-language and ME-language in the same sentence!

Be sure to keep your promises and take the initiative to do as you have promised. It will result in making you reliable as a parent and will help to strengthen the bond between the two of you in the long run.

When I return from work, I sit down with my daughter and use YOU-language to discover what is going on with her. Once I get a clear picture of her needs, still using YOU-language ("So you mean you want to play with me when you wake up in the morning?"), she will calm down and then we can work out TOGETHER a solution so that both of our needs get met.

The Difference between Needs and Solutions

Hunger is a need, whereas an apple, a lollipop, a cupcake, or some pasta are all solutions to satisfy that need. Celebrating is a need. Organizing a party at home, going to the movies, or spending money are all solutions to satisfy this need.

Please pay attention to the following: There's a big difference between negotiating on needs (also known as a compromise) and negotiating on solutions.

Let's imagine that I want to work because I have a need to earn money and my child wants to play the piano because she wants to relax—therefore making it impossible for me to concentrate on my work.

A compromise would be that I work for an hour and then she plays the piano for an hour, so we both get 50 percent of what we need.

Negotiating on solutions while not compromising our needs could mean that she can play the piano while I go to my office and work there.

Or it might mean that I work at home, and she watches a movie with earphones for relaxation instead of playing the piano.

When you negotiate on solutions, both of you will get 100 percent of what you need. Isn't that a wonderful idea? You need to be creative together to reach this goal. But the pay-off is phenomenal. Think of the lesson that your child will learn from this procedure. Your child will not only learn that his needs are very important, he will also learn that he needs to be considerate of others and THEIR needs.

CASE #5. It's not me who has difficulties communicating with our child; it's my partner who is struggling. What should I do?
I'm so glad you asked (smile). When your partner is struggling or your children are fighting with each other, your approach would be very similar: You don't have to do anything. To put it bluntly, it's not your problem, as your personal needs are not involved (unless they are screaming so loudly that you cannot hear the TV). Everybody is responsible for fulfilling their own needs.

However, there are some very helpful actions you could consider doing—for instance when your husband asks for your assistance or you notice that your children aren't getting anywhere with their rivalry. Your role would then be one of an intermediary, as you're helping the two parties to verbalize their problems, feelings, and needs. This way, you're helping the parties without having to side with anyone.

> "When you continue to kick against the chair leg, your father gets irritated."

When your child responds with "I like kicking the chair!" simply continue the conversation on your partner's behalf (unless your partner wants to pick it up from there) and use YOU-language first—"You enjoy moving your legs around, don't you?"—and then again state your partner's feelings or needs. "Your dad (or mom) dislikes the feeling which goes like BOOM . . . BOOM . . . BOOM."

Helping parties verbalize their needs and feelings will spark a learning process in them. And hopefully, one day, they will be able to make amends without your help.

CASE #6. When I enter my living room, I see my children fighting—again. Though my basic language is ME-language, in this case I want to start with YOU-language. This is the language I use when I want to offer my help.

In this case, my role is again a mediating one. After all, they are fighting with each other, not with me. I have a conflict with my child when our needs or our solutions are conflicting; the same is true when my child has a fight with their brother or sister. Because most children are not yet able to discuss their needs, I want to offer some help. Therefore, they will become aware of their own needs, and hopefully they will be able to resolve their own conflicts in the future. So my role is a mediating one. As a mediator, I follow the following guidelines:

1. I let them speak to each other.
2. I'm prepared for intense outbursts of emotions, and I use YOU-language to help them understand each other.
3. I let them generate their own solutions.
4. I never play the role of judge! I use ME-language to clarify this.

CASE #7. My child is using inappropriate words, both with his peers and with me. I want to share my feelings about that, using ME-language.

> "I really hate hearing words like that. It makes me feel very sad and uncomfortable."

Chances are that my child will not adjust his behavior simply because I dislike his words. In this example, do you notice that is it very hard for me to describe a specific outcome personally as a result of those inappropriate words? Whenever you fail to describe exact, concrete outcomes for you personally, your ME-language will have a low chance of resulting in change of behavior. After all, why does your child need to be considerate if there isn't any visible or concrete consequence?

Is there nothing one can do when children use inappropriate words? Well, first of all, assess your own vocabulary. Do you ever use inappropriate words yourself? Modeling is a very effective way of teaching kids values. But it doesn't work overnight. If a child says things they cannot tolerate, many parents will use their power (punishment or rewards) to make their child stop using those words. Remember, though, that using power will always jeopardize the quality of your relationship. Also realize that for most children, using inappropriate words is a phase they will outgrow. And last but not least, the more you forbid the use of certain behavior, the more your child may become attracted to display this behavior.

I also want to share with you a technique I used with my child when she was in the middle of that phase and used many inappropriate words. I explained in ME-language how I felt (very uncomfortable). At the same time, I used YOU-language to tell her that I recognized her need to fit in with her peers and her need to discover the world. Next we sat down and discussed a solution that worked very well for us: We all would use as many inappropriate words as we could think of in a five-minute time frame. Five minutes may seem like a short period of time. But I can assure you, it was very difficult to reach the five-minute mark altogether! Stopping was not allowed; we had to keep saying inappropriate words. Saying them at any other time during the day was not allowed either. Those were the rules we made together as a family in a democratic style.

And then some magic happened. At first my daughter laughed her head off, because her mom and dad were saying those forbidden words and she couldn't believe her ears! But then it was very difficult to keep going for five minutes! (You should try it for yourself, just for fun—after only a couple of minutes, it becomes very hard to come up with new words.) So after a few days, this activity was no fun anymore, and my child stopped saying the words. She now and then still uses words I prefer not to hear, but to be honest, I also use words now and then that are inappropriate. As long as she knows, just like I do, in which situation those words are considered inappropriate (i.e., at school, at her grandparents' dinner party, at a friend's house, etc.), it's not such a big deal to me.

CASE #8. My daughter is still a baby, but I can see her personality coming through. She has a strong will of her own. Now what do I do?

Remember that ME-language is your basic language. So, from an early age, start expressing your needs and feelings so your child learns more about you. Don't be afraid to talk to a child who cannot talk back yet. Children learn a lot of things by listening to you. You will not only strengthen the bond between the two of you because your baby will LOVE to hear your voice, you will also teach your baby new sounds and words as well. Sooner or later, your child will understand what you're saying, so don't worry. And yes, your child will discover her own ME. Good for her! I personally don't want to have a child who makes herself invisible because of others' demands. When the needs of your baby become visible, it's time to use a lot of YOU-language to discover her needs. Once you know her needs as well as your own, you should be able to figure out solutions that meet both of your needs. With small children, you may need to offer them different solutions, and as long as they're old enough, they will pick one. On the other hand, don't underestimate your child. Even young children, say two or three years old, may also be able to come up with solutions you have not thought of yourself. Remember that children who are involved in finding a solution will more easily commit themselves to the solution.

CASE #9. My son is five years old and refuses to eat the foods we offer him. He has made it into a power struggle, and I'm sick of it. I simply want to enjoy my meals and our time together. What should I do?

As always, ME-language is your basic language. So you express your need for harmony or peace and quiet or your need to enjoy family time. Furthermore, you express your sadness because the fighting interferes with your idea of harmony, peace and quiet, or enjoyment. "I'm feeling sad because I cannot enjoy my meal and I have a need for harmony." If you feel worried because your child eats too little, you express your worry: "I feel worried that you're not taking in enough nutrients."

Chances are, your son will stop fighting, but he still doesn't want to eat. Then what can you do? Whenever you feel the need to make a connection or don't know what to do next, try YOU-language and see what happens. Then you will know what's going on with your son, and you'll be able to combine your needs with his and come up with a solution that might work for both of you.

Children often use eating to battle with their parents. It's often the only means of power they can effectively use. Assess the dynamics around food in your home. Do you force your child to eat, therefore stimulating your child to rebel? Is eating fun in your home, even when there is no struggle going on? Is your child ever allowed to choose what to have for dinner? Is your child involved in preparing the meal? Personally, in the above case, I'd probably think that my son wants to tell me something. He's struggling with issues he cannot communicate differently. So I personally would want to help him and for that, I'd use a lot of YOU-language: "You don't feel like eating today?" or "You don't like the food I prepared?" It may or may not result in an eating child, but at least the fighting will have stopped. From there, using both YOU-language and ME-language could turn things around.

As you can see, in this case, change is not something you will accomplish overnight. Problems usually take time to emerge. They also take time to disappear. Don't worry if things don't seem to change yet after you first start a different approach. Believe in yourself and keep going!

CASE #10. My toddler keeps throwing things on the floor. This may seem like fun to him, but it is definitely not fun for me, because I need to clean up everything.

As we have learned, people behave because they are trying to fulfill their needs. Your toddler throws things on the floor because he has the need to play, to discover new things, to explore his world. So instead of thinking that he is intentionally bullying you, think of his needs. He wants to play and see what happens. Though ME-language is your basic language, your toddler might not be emotionally old enough to be considerate of others.

In this case, I would use ME-language to teach my child how I feel so he becomes considerate. I might say, "I am so busy—I don't have time to keep picking up your toys!" Besides ME-language, use a lot of YOU-language as well ("You really LOVE this game, don't you?") to connect with your child. Then, if throwing things is not acceptable to you, think of an alternative solution your toddler is allowed to do, such as throwing blocks in the hall or in his room.

CASE #11. My baby cries all day. I'm desperate!

Though babies are not well equipped yet as far as language is concerned, there is enough that we can do, especially using nonverbal language. First of all, babies cry because they want to send out a signal. They simply have no other means of communication. So first try to figure what your baby's need is. Does she need warmth? Milk? A clean diaper? Closeness? During this process, talk to her in YOU-language.

After all, you're trying to connect with your baby. "Are you feeling cold? Let me see, where's your blanket? That is why you're feeling cold—you have kicked away your blanket! Do you feel better now?" This way, your baby will learn your language. She LOVES to hear your voice anyway, and in the tonality you use, she will recognize your helping attitude. This might calm her down. If she is still crying and you have checked everything, and there is nothing more you can think of that you can do, consider that every person needs to discharge excess stress now and then. Make no mistake, no matter how well you take care of your child, your child will always build up stress. Feeling cold, alone, hungry, sleepy, or having too many stimuli will all cause a certain amount of stress. Allow your child to release her stress once in a while in the healthiest way possible: by crying. While your child is crying, stay with her, talk to her, and tell her it's OK to cry. "It's nice to have a good cry, don't you think? Go on, let it all out!" After all, crying does make people of all ages feel a lot better!

If you're still feeling worried about your baby's crying, please consult a specialist.

CASE #12. My teenager is out of control. He's into sex, drugs, tattoos, and the wrong friends. He seems to be living on his own planet. What can I do?

Well, first of all, I assume you have used a lot of ME-language in the past, because this is your basic language. The sooner you start using ME-language, the sooner you will benefit from using it. So, from the time your child is young, preferably from birth, start using ME-language.

Children are more easily influenced before they hit puberty. Once you find yourself in the above situation, please realize that your teen will not listen to your well-intended advice.

He has shut you off from his world, and now you'd like to reconnect. Connecting is something we do with YOU-language. Not judging anyone is important in any human relationship. Not judging your teen is crucial in order to survive! Use a lot of YOU-language to find an opening into his life. You might say, "You look as if you had a good time with your friends." As always, don't expect things to change overnight. If your teen doesn't want to talk, respect that and don't try to force him to talk with you. Forcing communication will only increase the gap between you.

I will make one exception: When there is real danger involved (to his health or even his life), I'd use POWER to force my child out of the situation. My child who's addicted to drugs will be forced by me to go to a clinic.

CASE #13. I don't have any real issues yet, but in general I want to protect my child from the cruel world. But how?
First of all, reflect on your own beliefs and convictions. If you think the world is cruel, this belief will influence the way you speak and act. You are a role model for your child. If you think the world is a beautiful place, these beliefs will also influence the way you speak and behave. Either way, be aware of the implicit messages you're sending to your child.

There are parents who want to protect their children from as many things, especially bad things, as possible. On the other hand, there are also parents who don't protect their children from anything. Neither way is effective. As a parent, I have a different perspective: I want my child to make as many mistakes as she needs. Making mistakes is a powerful way to learn lessons. Of course, safety provided. I use ME-language to tell about my personal experiences ("I have seen/experienced how easy/difficult it is to get a job with/without having a diploma" or "I feel awkward walking in a dark alley all alone, because I don't know who's following me"). Then it's up to my child. If she still wants to take the hard route, let her. Of course, again, safety provided. If she wants to go to a school below her capabilities simply because she has friends there, let her. She can always mend the pieces afterwards. Will it be easy? No, of course not! But hey, your child chose the hard way herself, didn't she? The lessons learned will be invaluable. Instead of protecting your child from everything you fear, be there for her in case she needs you, and then use YOU-language ("You think that school is too easy for you?").

CASE #14. My child doesn't pick up his clothes. His bedroom is a mess, and it drives me crazy!

As always, start by expressing ME-language; after all, it drives *you* crazy, not him! "Seeing those clothes scattered all over the place drives me crazy! I need to give my head a break." Express your ME-language as authentically as possible. Hopefully this will result in a change of behavior. After all, this is YOUR need, not his.

Also, realize that your child behaves because he also has needs. He probably has the need to relax, or the need to be on time for school made him decide to throw his clothes on the floor. Either way, once you have expressed your ME-language and your child doesn't seem to respond or doesn't seem to care, switch to YOU-language to find out what's going on ("You seem unaware" or "It looks like you don't care. Is that the case?" Then, go back to ME-language and make clear how it affects YOU. "I understand that you are tired in the morning, but I need an extra ten minutes to collect all the clothes when I want to wash them. I don't have that much time." Keep switching between YOU-language and ME-language for as long as it is needed. However, keep in mind that your child may give precedence to his own need. Are you willing to accept that? If not, pick a peaceful, quiet moment to talk with him about your issue and together with your child, try to think of a solution in which both your needs are being satisfied.

CASE #15. My child doesn't want to go to school in the morning. Therefore I'm late for work.

As always, use ME-language to say that you want to be on time, because you have an appointment at work, or you have made a promise to be on time every day.

If this doesn't result in a change of behavior, or your child keeps saying she does not want to go to school, pick a peaceful, quiet moment and use YOU-language to find out what's going on with her. You might be surprised by the things you hear. "You don't like going to school, right?"

The child may respond by saying: "No, I HATE school!" There is clearly a significant amount of emotion there, so you respond by saying, "Wow, you really despise school that much?" Chances are that your child will say something like "Well, in fact it's the stupid teacher I hate. She always talks to Casey, but totally ignores me!" Now you're getting somewhere! It seems that your child has the unmet need to be seen. If you check this assumption, and continue to use YOU-language, your child will not only tell you what's going on, but will start emotionally processing this experience as well. Talking to you about their issue might be the trigger they need to do something about it themselves. In other cases, your child may not be ready yet (let them take charge of this process as long as their behavior is not interfering with your needs) or will ask you for help. Now that you know what the root cause is of the clinging, it will be so much easier to solve the problem!

CASE #16. My child is clinging to me. He doesn't want me to leave.

In this case, your child has an issue, so I would use YOU-language to discover what is going on. If you want your child to tell you his deepest thoughts, fears, and needs, remember to use YOU-language, which never contains judgments, solutions, or advice of any kind. If your child chooses not to tell you anything, I'm sorry, but so be it.

Never think your child doesn't appreciate your nonjudgmental attitude, because believe me, your child will still benefit from all the great things YOU-language has to offer. Your child will decide when the time is right to invite you into his world. Be prepared for that moment.

CASE #17. My child does not tell me anything.

As in the situation above, I would definitely try to use YOU-language over a longer period of time. And be prepared for the magical moment when your child decides to let you in.

Remember, in any situation, DO NOT mix ME-language and YOU-language in one sentence. It will make your message BLURRY. Avoid sentences like: "I want YOU to greet me when you enter my living room." In this sentence, ME language ("I want and need respect") and YOU-language are mixed up ("You're in a hurry?"). Thus, this is an ambiguous message.

Exercise

I'd like you to get out a notebook and briefly describe cases where communication between you and your child was rocky. The case studies I've described have come from real families dealing with real issues. I'm sure some of them triggered situations that have occurred in your family. Jot down ten of these situations and think of how you would approach them in the future.

In the next chapter I am going to share the reasons some parents fail while others get ahead. This will tie up a lot of loose ends, fit all the pieces together, and refine your communication with your child.

CHAPTER 12
HOW TO STAY AHEAD OF THE GAME

"Do not wait for leaders; do it alone, person to person."
MOTHER TERESA

CONGRATULATIONS TO YOU! The number of people who actually make it to the end of a book is fairly small. Because you're still here, I know you really want to be the parent who brings out the best in their children, and you want to do everything you possibly can so your life, your child's life, and our world starts improving. That makes me really sure that you care. You care for your child. You care for yourself, and you care about your relationship with your child. On top of that, our world will benefit too, as the ripple effect will be astonishing. I admire your determination and I'm so proud of you—honestly!

I'm so happy you're still here, because I simply know by now how dedicated you are to turning your upbringing into successful parenting. You know, very few parents ever think about the parenting system they are using. Even fewer parents decide that the system they already know is not serving them, their children, or our world for that matter. They realize their children need something else to make sure they will receive the level of acceptance, support, and inspiration every child deserves. And of those few parents, even fewer parents take the step to DO something about it. YOU are one of those special few. Congratulations on being part of that select group.

Now that I have explained the whole system, it is time to fit all the pieces together. In this chapter I'm going to tell you the things you still want to hear: the last puzzle pieces, as it were.

In the previous chapter, we covered how to apply ME-language and YOU-language to different situations. In this chapter, I'm going to tell you why some parents fail while others succeed at using this system effectively. But first, please realize that acquiring new skills evolves through different stages:

1. Unconsciously incompetent. In this first stage, you are not aware of the fact that you are incompetent in using the new skills. You may or may not experience problems on this topic. This may be the case when you constantly fight with your child, and even though you wish things were different, you don't have a clue as to what you could do differently.

2. Consciously incompetent. In this stage, you are aware of the things you still don't know and therefore don't apply. This may be the case when you realize that fighting with your child happens when you forget to connect to his feelings.

Instead, you keep using ME-language (or worse: you mix both ME-language and YOU-language), and you realize you should take another approach, but you haven't mastered the skills yet to use them effectively. This stage sucks for most people! You want to do things differently. You now know how to do it. The only thing is that you're still incompetent! I totally understand that this stage is frustrating and uncomfortable. The main focus for this stage is to keep going, because there is no other way to become better at something! As Michael Jordan once said: "I have failed over and over and over in my life. And that is why I succeeded."

3. Consciously competent. In this stage, you are refining your parenting skills. You're improving your skills all the time! In some cases, you have experienced how well you've been able to apply your newly acquired skills! You have had your first number of successes and you're excited about it—and you should be! Now that you are aware of the situations where you should apply your new skills, your confidence grows by the day.

4. Unconsciously competent. You have become so proficient at parenting that things go well for you without you realizing it anymore! You use the skills unconsciously on a daily basis and you don't even have to think about when you should use them and when you'd better NOT use them. You have reached your desired goals and are enjoying them without having to think about your skills anymore!

If you're wondering how fast you will go through the different stages, please realize that this is dependent on one thing and one thing only: your commitment!

I have worked with hundreds of parents, teaching them this approach. I have extensive experience myself using ME-language and YOU-language. I do not intend to brag or to give the impression that I am perfect myself, because I'm definitely NOT (you can ask both my husband and my child!). However, I have seen and heard what people do and do NOT do and the result of their doing (or not doing). So I now have a clear idea of the reasons why some parents fail and others get ahead. I would love for you to profit from my knowledge and experience so you can avoid the pitfalls!

1. Keep your focus on needs and feelings and negotiate on solutions. Always search for ways both parties can be satisfied. Once the needs of your child and your own needs are clear, you can both search for solutions that satisfy both of your needs.

For example: Your son always makes a mess in the kitchen when he comes home from school. When you want to start preparing dinner, you need to clean up his mess first. This costs you time and energy. You're sick and tired of doing that on a daily basis. You have used ME-language to clarify your own needs: You have a need to relax, and you have a need to spend your time wisely. Using YOU-language, you have discovered his needs: his need to eat and his need to relax. Although you have now identified both of your needs, there is no solution yet. He keeps messing up the kitchen and you are still frustrated about the time and energy you waste on cleaning up his mess every day. Persisting in ME-language is not getting you anywhere.

Now the time has come to ask your son to sit down for a moment with you when you both are feeling relaxed. Discuss the needs you both have. Clarify in ME-language that the current solution (his making something to eat after school) does not work for you because it interferes with your needs. Discuss possible alternative solutions so both your needs and his needs are met. For example, you prepare a snack in the morning for your son and put it in the fridge for him to eat when he comes home from school. Or he prepares his own snack someplace else and will clean it up while you're preparing dinner. It does not matter what solution both of you choose. The important thing is that neither one of you has to compromise his own needs. On top of that: both needs are met. Keep in mind that when you focus on needs, you never have to judge your child. In this case, your child is hungry, instead of messy. You have focused on needs and negotiated on solutions.

2. Keep going! Your child needs a role model. Your child needs YOU just as much as they need the other parent. For a healthy development, both parents are needed. You cannot delegate these skills to your partner just because your partner is proficient in these skills. Your child needs YOU as well. No matter what he says or does, your ongoing efforts to invest in a healthy relationship with your child will ALWAYS be needed—no matter what age your child is. Your child may be an adult, but they will always want you to invest in the relationship. Make no mistake about that!

Do NOT, under any circumstances, give up on using the skills you have learned in this program! Many people dive into a system and expect a miracle to happen overnight. Is it possible to lose a hundred pounds in a week? No, of course not! Is it possible to become world's best runner in three weeks? No, of course not! Is it possible to fully integrate new skills in two months? No, of course not. Skills take time to integrate into one's system. Do not expect to become 100 percent perfect, because this is impossible.

Let's face it. We're all human. Do not judge yourself for making mistakes; after all, we all learn by experience! You started this program for a reason, and every bit of progress you make is a change for the better. Never expect to become 100 percent perfect.

Instead, compare it to a diet. What I have shared with you

is the best possible diet for you. Does that mean that eating a piece of chocolate once a week is going to hurt you? Of course not! As long as your basic diet is healthy, you'll be fine. It's a different story when you eat chocolates three times a day over a longer period of time. The same is true for this program. Mistakes are part of human nature, so don't be ashamed to show who you are to your child. Be proud of who you are, including your best qualities and your shortcomings. It will allow your child to feel comfortable about his or her flaws as well.

One note: Making a mistake is one thing, but how do you deal with the consequences? Whenever I make mistakes, I apologize to my child and explain (using ME-language) what my intentions were and what I should have done. Together we discuss what we can do in the future so a similar situation can be avoided.

Keep practicing. As with all new skills, reading about them or hearing about them is not enough. You will need to practice, practice, and practice to master them! Don't be afraid to take your time to invest in your relationship. Yes, this approach may take up more time than simply ordering your kid to do something; the payoff, on the other hand, is HUGE, both in time saved in future engagements and in the quality of your relationship and the ripple effect in our world.

Keep a journal and write down the changes you have seen. You don't have to write every day. Once every couple of days or once a week is fine. Also, if you're not a writer, you can also use voice memo or reflect with your partner or friend. It doesn't matter which vehicle you choose, as long as you find a way to stay focused and motivated.

Rely on your common sense. Don't do or say things that make you feel stupid. Don't do things that don't make sense to you. This approach assumes congruency. Your inside feelings should match your outward behavior. Also, remember that in the beginning, communicating like this may feel awkward, but you will get used to it once you do it more often.

Continue your daily life. You don't have to use ME-language and YOU-language all the time, but using the languages as much as possible will get you further than you've ever thought possible! If you want to ask your child where he left his sports clothes, don't freak out about trying to say things in ME-language. Yes, it is possible to ask questions in ME-language, as in: "Honey, where are your sports clothes? I want to wash them." As you can see, the sentence in ME-language does add some extra information and will probably stimulate your son more to help you out than if you shouted at him: "Where are your sports clothes?" But if you forget to add that extra sentence, and he responds by answering your question, who cares about that extra sentence? He may also ask you why you want to know that. In that case, that's your key for using ME-language. So don't panic because you're supposed to say things differently. Read this book again from time to time so you will remember the things you've learned, and you will know how to progress from there.

Always make an effort to improve the quality of the relationship with your child. Your child is worth it. And so are you. I know there are many children going through rough times. Their parents are in the middle of a divorce, or their brother or sister is sick, or they are being bullied at school, or they want to make friends with somebody but that person does not reciprocate their feelings. There are many different reasons why children are feeling mental pain. I know how painful it can be to see your child going through difficult phases. I also know that most people, children included, will not show their pain openly; they will probably close themselves off from kindness, love, and warmth. It is their effort to protect themselves from further pain and suffering. They will also refrain from showing love, warmth, and care for others—you included.

This all may lead to a situation where your child seems distant, rebellious, or reluctant. Make no mistake! Seeming not to care doesn't mean that they don't. Seeming distant doesn't mean that they don't have a need to feel connection. Or love. Or warmth. Every single human being needs acceptance, support, and inspiration. Every single one! This is especially true when your child is going through a hard time. Simply by continuing your efforts in reaching out and connecting, your child will ultimately feel your intentions. You will be grateful that you persevered. And so will your child. Once better times lie ahead for you both, your child will think back to those times when you never, ever gave up on him. The lesson learned is invaluable. The implicit message of behavior like this is that your child is worth you making an effort. In the end, he will never give up on himself either. He will take care of himself and the loved ones around him with acceptance, support, and inspiration. Isn't that the ultimate message you want for your child?

If you feel you need more support in learning the desired skills, please check my website, laurafobler.com, and see if there's a program available to assist you further. If not, please contact me and tell me how I can help you on your journey. I always enjoy hearing from parents, and I'm open 24/7!

3. Put the system aside only when you don't see any other way. Use your power (punishment, reward) when it's absolutely necessary—as in life-or-death situations. When my child almost gets run over by a car, I'm not thinking of YOU-language or ME-language; I simply grab her and pull her away. This is power, because there is no democracy whatsoever involved. It's also a matter of life and death. I don't think running late for school falls in the same category! However, if you need to use power, I strongly urge you to apologize afterwards, because this does not align with your overall approach. Use YOU-language to reconnect ("Pulling you like that must have freaked you out, didn't it?") and try to think of a way you can prevent a similar situation from happening, preferably together with your child. She will appreciate your efforts to improve your behavior and will be happy to contribute to a solution.

4. Apply this approach to yourself as well. Do NOT second guess yourself by judging yourself. The same will happen to your child when you judge him. Let go of the idea that you have done a good job or a bad job. You have made an effort. That counts! That counts for just as much as a perfect job. Honestly! Your child will be tolerant as long as you continue your efforts. Don't be afraid to make mistakes. After all, we live in a world of duality. There is no dark without light; no small without big; no mountain without a valley; and no success without mistakes. Keep trying and you WILL succeed! And so what if your child notices that you are practicing? What a great message this would be—that learning these skills implies that you're not perfect. Let your child know that you are willing to learn new things. It also implies that you're taking responsibility for the situation, regardless of the status quo. YOU have decided to do something about it instead of blaming another person. What a powerful message this is!

5. Share this system with everyone around you! Do NOT limit the use of this system on your child only. Share it with everyone! You can practice and use it on anyone. Don't hesitate to try some YOU-language on your patients, your clients, your students, your manager, your parents, the girl in the shop, or your partner! The more you practice, the sooner you will see results. At the same time, I urge you to let others take responsibility for their own learning. Don't pressure anyone into learning things they don't want to learn, because if they don't want to learn it, they will not learn it. Period. If you want your child to copy your way of communicating, don't worry—your child will copy you sooner or later simply because you have shown your child the way, and eventually your child will use it. Trust the process!

Let's recap where we have been:

- Keep your focus on needs and feelings. If necessary, negotiate on solutions.
- Keep going at all times. Your child, you, and the world are worth the effort.
- Set the system aside only when you see no other way.
- Apply the system to yourself as well.
- Share the system with everyone around you!

After having covered the five big DOs that will set you apart from the rest, let's cover some FAQs in the next chapter. These answers might help you along on your journey.

CHAPTER 13
FAQS

"If the inner world is inundated with peace, then the nightmare of world war cannot even come into being."

SRI CHINMOY

I OFTEN HEAR the same questions over and over, so before you start implementing this program, please take a close look at these frequently asked questions, as they might give you the answer you're looking for yourself or fill in any open gaps!

Q: I do as you tell me to, but it doesn't seem to work. What am I doing wrong?

A: Well, this isn't a miracle solution that works overnight. If you cannot see a result, that doesn't mean there is no result or that you're doing anything wrong. Things may change on the inside of your child. As long as you stick to the basic rules and refrain from harmful behavior such as (corporal) punishment, smacking, or name calling, have faith in what you're doing and trust things will have an effect, sooner or later.

Q: Things seem to have gotten out of control in our home. I'm not the authoritative type at all, but my children have taken over; they now control everything. How do I turn this around?

A: Sometimes, when parents are not very dominant, kids take the chance to take control, and this may end up becoming a situation where THEY control everything and their parents obey. It's like a reversed world. In this case, you may find it very difficult to implement the strategies I have discussed in this program. Not because it is impossible, but because children who have taken over everything will not give up their power easily. In this case, using power (punishment and/or rewards) might just be the tool you need to restore a distorted situation. Mind you, I'm not enthusiastic about any power system using punishment and rewards, but rewarding your child for so-called "good" behavior may just be the trick you need. Once you're on speaking terms again, introduce ME-language and YOU-language as soon as possible, and get rid of all power methods!

Q: I'm in the middle of a conversation and suddenly I don't know what to say or what to do. What can I do?

A: In ANY situation, if you're lost for a strategy, try YOU-language to connect or re-connect and pick it up from there.

Q: My child does not behave the way I want her to, despite ME-language and YOU-language. What do I do now?

A: Depending on the situation, there are different reasons why ME-language does not work. For one, are your ME-messages strong enough? Do you say, "I don't like what I see," or do you say, "Seeing that scares the hell out of me because it makes me afraid. I need to pay money to buy a new couch."

Reflect on your ME-messages and see how you can make a stronger impact.

Second, have you used YOU-language as well to listen to your child? And third, do you really want your child to obey you all the time? Remember, people behave because they are trying to fulfill their needs. The same goes for your child. If your child does not respond to your ME-language and YOU-language and carries on with the undesired behavior, question what need she is trying to fulfill. And see if you can find a solution together that works for both of your needs. In some cases your child will continue doing things you will not like. In that case, think of your own youth. Did you do things your parents didn't approve of? Did it stop you from doing them? Please realize that condemning your child's behavior will only increase the gap between you. Use YOU-language to re-connect. You may be surprised, because the more you use YOU-language, the more understanding you will get of your child and her motives.

In case you're using ME-language and YOU-language over a longer period of time and not seeing any difference AT ALL and you're worried about your child's behavior, consider consulting a professional.

Furthermore, another reason your child may ignore how you feel is that there is no tangible consequence for you to verbalize with ME-language. For example: When your child has painted her hair green and you hate the way she looks, what can you do besides saying, "I don't like that color. I feel uncomfortable walking next to you."

If I were your child, to be honest, I couldn't care less about your thoughts, and I'd keep my green hair. If this sounds like a familiar example in your own home, I invite you to research your values and question yourself. Are you are allowing your child to be who she wants to be? What harm does she do to anyone if she dyes her hair green? Or purple? Or gets herself a Mohawk?

If, on the other hand, the green stuff she put in her hair came from my bottle and now my bottle is empty, that would probably impress her more, because now I can say that her behavior costs me money. Always remember that the more tangible the consequence is for you personally, the better results you will have with ME-language. If your child still doesn't respond to your ME-language, try using YOU-language to discover what's going on with your child.

Q: Things are going very well now. Is it safe to stop using ME-language or YOU-language and get back to normal?

A: As tempting as it may seem, please do not stop using ME-language or YOU-language. Using these languages will make the bond between you and your child stronger every day. Strengthening your connection will make the relationship resilient and will make you less vulnerable to incidents you didn't expect. You will soon notice how quickly and easily conflicts are resolved once you have established a firm connection between you and your child. As an experienced user of this system, I can tell you that I rarely have conflicts with my child, and when we do, they are resolved in a heartbeat!

Q: I am using both ME-language and YOU-language and things are going well as far as the technical side is concerned. Unfortunately, I still experience conflicts (i.e., conflicting needs) once in a while. How is that possible?

A: Though we all would love to live in a world without conflicting solutions, this is impossible to achieve. Where people live together, conflicts will be there. Always. You and I may have the same need for rest, but we usually have different solutions to fulfill that need. I may want to listen to music, and you may want to meditate in silence. This situation could easily lead to a conflict. But if we focus on the underlying need (rest), it is quite easy to see how everyone needs rest. We can work out a solution that works for both of us, such as meditating with earphones, or listening to music with earphones, or reading and meditating in separate rooms. Conflicts are fights over solutions. After all, we all have similar needs.

See for yourself. Do different countries battle each other over needs, such as the need to rest, the need for safety, or the need to feel free? No, they battle over solutions, such as the borders of countries, religions, or the amount of women! As far as your relationship with your child is concerned, it is not the amount of conflicts that define the quality of your relationship. It is the way you approach conflicts that defines the quality of your relationship. Are you persisting in using ME-language to get your way, thereby neglecting your child? Or are you using YOU-language as a means to research how your child thinks and feels? Are you searching for ways for both of your needs to be satisfied? After you've used this approach for some time, you will realize that conflicts will be settled more easily because your child now knows you take him and his needs seriously.

Q: I'm very enthusiastic about this approach. My partner is NOT, unfortunately. What should I do?
A: This is an issue that happens often, believe me. Many people have been raised by the traditional power approach

(punishment/rewards). This is the only approach they know. I applaud you for taking this step without the support of your partner. It will be a long and winding road if you're alone. The ideal situation is where both parents are using this system. However, if only one parent uses the system, your child will benefit. I know it is hard, but please, never try to convince others with this approach. Believe me, I've been there; it will NOT work. On the contrary, it will probably lead to greater conflict. You may have experienced that already.

Instead, use YOU-language with your partner as a way to reconnect. Eventually, most partners will see that this approach leads to better results. And yes, this WILL take time.

Q: This is very exciting and interesting stuff! Where can I read more?

A: If you find these ideas and concepts interesting, I suggest you continue your journey with books from authors such as Carl Rogers, Thomas Gordon, Marshall Rosenberg, or Haim Ginott. I can also highly recommend books by Aletha Solter and Alfie Kohn. I realize that I'm not giving enough credit to others who have done great work as well. Go out and explore. I have given you some names of relevant authors to start with. With the list of resources, you should be able to find your way.

And yes, you're absolutely right! Learning a new language is NOT an easy task.

Your accent will be audible forever, but if you persevere, soon your child will become a native speaker. As Haim Ginott once put it: "Children are like wet cement. Whatever falls on them makes an impression." So please, for all our sakes, don't give up!

CONCLUSION

"Human beings, indeed all sentient beings, have the right to pursue happiness and live in peace and freedom."
DALAI LAMA

WOW, WHAT A journey this has been! I'm so grateful for the time I got to spend with you. I'm grateful for your dedication and for taking the time to actually read this book. The good news is that by now you should have a reasonable idea of how this system works . . . in theory. Now you can start to put into practice everything that you learned so far and continue learning about your child and yourself! From personal experience, I can honestly say that I'm still on this learning journey myself, and I'm truly hoping to continue this journey for the rest of my life, because I really love deepening the relationship between my child and myself.

Before I tell you what to do first now that you have almost finished the book, I'd like to refresh your memory and briefly summarize what we've covered.

I started out telling you how vulnerable I felt as a parent, wishing for my child to be safe in this world forever. However, our world is in turmoil. Our world has been caught in a so-called power loop: individual people, groups of people, and/or nations often use power in an effort to control others. Unfortunately, the use of power usually has devastating effects, as there are three ways in which people respond to power:

1. Fleeing from power, such as running away from home, abusing alcohol, lying, or committing suicide.

2. Fighting against power: aggressive behavior or conspiring against the power source.

3. Submitting to power. The subdued emotions that come along with this option are usually not immediately visible.

None of these responses is helpful for the victim, as victims always defer their own needs one way or the other, often leaving them with all sorts of negative feelings. If needs and feelings are ignored over a long period of time, there is a good chance that people will become emotionally and psychologically damaged, with all kinds of consequences. History has proven this statement, unfortunately. Only during the eighteenth century, when philosophers such as Jean-Jacques Rousseau promoted the idea that children are not miniature grown-ups but individual creatures with needs, wants, and feelings, did thinking about children in general start to shift.

Conclusion

Even though many parents now recognize that murdering or abusing their own child is not the smartest thing to do, they still do not think twice about using a power system to control their children, completely oblivious of the consequences. Children who have been brought up like this are at risk of becoming violent, aggressive, or destructive people!

If we want to eradicate all escalated conflict from our planet, we need an approach to parenting that shies away from all power and thus inequality; instead, we need to take all emotions and needs from all parties into consideration.

If we don't pay attention to the negative experiences and the accompanying negative emotions we all endure during our lives, we will never process our emotions effectively. This is a serious risk, as emotionally damaged people tend to have all sorts of problems; becoming an aggressive adult is one of them. As a society, we can offer therapy to affected unfortunate individuals who need help in order to heal. However, wouldn't it be much easier to help our children process their emotions effectively during their youth so they stay healthy forever, thus preventing aggression in the first place? Our society already spends so much money on helping troubled citizens, while it would be so much easier and cheaper to prevent them!

I spent a lot of time researching psychological books and programs that promote equality between parents and children and take emotions into consideration. I have analyzed and synthesized all the information into this seven-step program so you can help your child become an emotionally healthy individual who will never participate in aggressive or violent behavior!

Step One: Everybody is responsible for their own needs.
Step Two: Refrain from judging.
Step Three: Never punish or reward.
Step Four: Being consistent is impossible and unnecessary.
Step Five: Trust that your child will want to show their best behavior.
Step Six: Use ME-language.
Step Seven: Use YOU-language.

Your First Actions

You might be wondering what your first action should be once you finish reading this book. I suggest you start re-reading the book and start implementing ME-language into your daily life and just see what happens! When you're comfortable using ME-language, gradually introduce YOU-language as well, so you will be able to handle complicated conflicts while also dealing with your own emotions. This way, you will not get overwhelmed by anyone's emotions, and you will experience progression in your learning journey!

Before we part ways, let me share one more story with you. Years ago, when my daughter attended primary school, we had to drive her to school. My husband took her to school in the morning before work, while I picked her up from school in the afternoon after work. When I picked her up from school, a diversity of moms and dads flocked to the school premises, waiting for their offspring to finally evacuate the school building. I usually saw the same moms and dads every day, and the parents who were waiting were a variety of all kinds of human beings. Some were tall; some were tiny. Some were fat, some were skinny, some were young, some were old, and so forth. This was nothing special, as one can see such a mix of people almost anywhere in the world. However, there was one mother in particular who caught my attention. She was not very tall, yet she was quite muscular with a very athletic, almost masculine gait to her. She had a very modern haircut, and her hair was dyed black. She also wore quite heavy makeup. While I do not always wear makeup myself, I had never seen her without makeup. I was not the only person who was riveted by her appearance; I saw many parents staring at her. Even though I never spoke to her while I was waiting for my child, I noticed her almost every day.

One day I received a phone call from a parent who wanted to attend one of my parenting classes. As I asked her how she had found me, what class she wanted to take, and so forth, she told me that she and her significant other wanted to attend my parenting class as a couple, and she said that they already knew me because they saw me every day at school waiting for my child. At that point, I still had no idea who they were, but that changed soon enough.

When my new parenting class was just about to start, two ladies entered the classroom. One of them was the woman I had been fascinated with, even though at that point I had no idea why. Her name was Judy. During the eight sessions I had with this group, it became clear to me that Judy had endured some real difficulties during her life. She requested a time-out on several occasions, as the exercises I offered the group were too distressing to her. Over the weeks, humbleness took the better part of me. The woman I was captivated by appeared to be such a sweetheart, someone who was simply damaged by the experiences she had had in her life. I suddenly realized where my ambiguous feeling was coming from every time I saw her, that sense of being intrigued by her appearance. It was clear to me that her warm personality, which I got a glimpse of through the way she looked at me, did not match her appearance, which I would call a bit rough or even rowdy. I was shocked when I realized this, as I finally got the picture. This woman had endured so many difficulties in her life, heard so many judgments from other people (maybe even her own?), and experienced so much non-acceptance that she probably had built up a defensive wall by the way she presented herself to the world. It made absolute sense to me.

I feel that one of the most powerful experiences of my parenting class is that I treat participants exactly the same way as I instruct them to treat their children. That means that everybody is responsible for their own needs, and I never judge my participants, not even by saying "Well done!" after they have completed an exercise. I do not use punishments or rewards; I give them an honest insight in my own needs and feelings; I trust their best intentions; and I use ME-language and YOU-language as often as I can.

At the end of the whole course, I always ask for honest feedback and have the participants fill out an evaluation form. I want to know what the participants picked up from the course, what they found helpful in particular, what they suggest I change, and much more. I'm also very interested in knowing their biggest takeaway from the course. The response some parents give after going through the course is astonishing, such as: "Thank you so much for reminding me that my child has feelings too. It honestly never even crossed my mind." I'm always humbled by sentences like this, because I apparently succeeded in letting those participants see and feel the world through the eyes of another human being—their own child—which from my perspective is a very helpful approach toward resuming peace. I always get stoked when I read responses like this; they truly inspire me to spread my message to as many people as possible. If parents are not aware of the fact that their children have feelings too, how can they expect their children to be aware of other people's feelings?

Judy's response on the evaluation form was a relatively short sentence, but the impact her words had on me was substantial. When I read her response, my heart instantly melted, and I felt my eyes tearing up. At once, I found myself in her shoes and realized how life must have been for her. After reading this, I can clearly remember my sheer determination to never, ever, judge people again. The simple sentence Judy wrote down in response to this last question said it all:

"Thank you for letting me be who I am."

You Can Do This!

I'm impressed; I really am. You took the time to read all the previous chapters, allowing me to explain everything about the seven steps, and now here we are. You and I have come such a long way together! That's an indication to me how committed you are to improve your situation! Whether you want to improve your situation at home or the situation in our world is irrelevant. You want things to be different; you took action, and I applaud you for that! You've definitely overcome the first hurdle, which is to read everything I have to say about the seven steps.

Again, I'd like to encourage you to have a close look at all the necessary steps while applying ME-language as often as you can. Will you be able to get it right immediately? Probably not! Will you fail more often than you will succeed? I guess so! It is likely that you will fail many times. So did I when I first started. Don't let this discourage you. I urge you to keep going, because sooner or later, you will definitely succeed—and then watch what happens! Also, at first you may succeed one time out of a hundred, but if you stay determined, I guarantee that this number will rise. Will you ever be able to reach a success score of one hundred out of one hundred occasions? Probably not! But don't worry, I wouldn't be able to make that number either, even if I wanted to! Fortunately, that shouldn't be a problem at all. It shows that you and I are humans, made of flesh and blood, and we cannot score a perfect ten all the time—and that's fine. This way, our children see that we make mistakes too and that it is perfectly fine to make them, and thus they will feel comfortable when they make mistakes of their own. Also, it won't hurt your child when you make mistakes now and then. As long as your foundation is solid and you know how to repair any unforeseen damage, there's no need to panic.

Never lose sight of the end goal! Can you imagine a world in which people are using ME-language and YOU-language all

Conclusion

the time, therefore accepting, supporting, and inspiring others continuously? I can beyond any doubt! I do not at all have a negative perspective of the world we all are living in. I can see how many good, decent, hardworking people are living on this planet. People who want to learn new things to improve their life, their situation, and the world. People like you. The fact that you're still here with me is enough of an indication to me of how devoted you are to changing our world. And when you start to change your private world, your child's world will change as well. And so will his friends' world. It's a ripple effect. By exhibiting the courage to learn a new perspective, you have taken the first step to improving your situation.

I know for sure that this approach will lead to less conflict, more happiness, more bonding, more connection, more love, and a better relationship with your child. Ultimately this approach will also lead us to a world free of conflict. Using the skills I have taught you, you will be able to prevent a lot of problems and contribute to world peace, starting in your very own home!

You WILL make a difference—not just in the life of your child. This carries on further than you have ever anticipated. Your child will hopefully remember his upbringing for the rest of his life and will treat his siblings and peers the same way. It will improve his relationship with the adults with whom he's going to be involved once he's grown up. Think of your grandchildren who will also benefit! Your efforts at this point have the power to touch hundreds and hundreds of people. Wouldn't that be the greatest gift—not only to yourself, but also to your child and to our world? And trust me, *you can do this!*

I'd love to hear from you! Tell me about the changes you

have accomplished in your life. I'd love to hear your struggles too, so I can improve this system in a way that will serve you and many others in the future. Even if you don't have something specific to tell me, I'd love to hear from you anyhow. Really. You can reach me any time at info@laurafobler.com.

Having said this, I wish you all the best. And who knows, maybe one day you and I will meet personally—in a world free from conflict.

"You may say I'm a dreamer, but I'm not the only one. I hope someday you'll join us. And the world will live as one."
— John Lennon

RESOURCES

Adams, L., and Lenz, E. 1989. *Be Your Best: Personal Effectiveness in Your Life and Your Relationships.* New York: Perigee Books.

Convention on the Rights of the Child; https://en.wikipedia.org/wiki/Convention_on_the_Rights_of_the_Child.

d'Ansembourg, Thomas. 2007. *Being Genuine: Stop Being Nice, Start Being Real.* Encinitas, California: PuddleDancer Press.

Dreikurs, R. 1964. *Children: The Challenge.* New York: Plume.

Frankl, V. 1959. *Man's Search for Meaning.* Boston: Beacon Press.

Ginott, H. 1965. *Between Parent and Child.* New York: Three River Press.

Gordon, T. 1975. *Parent Effectiveness Training.* New York: Penguin Books

Gordon, T. 1977. *Leader Effectiveness Training.* New York: Perigee.

Gordon, T. 1989. *Teaching Children Self-Discipline.* New York: Times Books.

Gordon, T., and Burch, N. 1974 *Teacher Effectiveness Training: The Proven Program to Help Teachers Bring Out the Best in Students of All Ages.* New York: David McKay Company.

Grille, R. 2008. *Parenting for a Peaceful World.* Richmond, UK: The Children's Project.

Hendsbee, D. 2015. What's changed in air travel since 1960? https://www.iamat.org/blog/whats-changed-in-air-travelsince-1960/ April 18, 2017.

Henriques, G. 2017. Understanding emotions and how to process them. The adaptive and maladaptive processing of emotions https://www.psychologytoday.com/blog/theory-knowledge/201701/understanding-emotions-and-how-process-them May 22, 2017.

International Monetary Fund, April 18, 2017; http://www.imf.org/external/pubs/ft/fandd/2014/09/kose.htm.

Jenson, J. 1996. *Reclaiming Your Life. A Step-By-Step Guide to Using Regression Therapy to Overcome the Effects of Childhood Abuse.* New York: Penguin Putnam.

Kohn, A. 2005. *Unconditional Parenting: Moving from Rewards and Punishments to Love and Reason.* New York: Atria Books.

Kohn, A. 1996. *Punished by Rewards: The Trouble with Gold Stars, Incentive Plans, A's, Praise, and Other Bribes.* Boston: Houghton Mifflin.

Kohn A. 1996. *Beyond Discipline: From Compliance to Community.* Alexandria, Virginia: ASCD.

Kose, M., and Ozturk, E. 2014. A World of Change, *Finance & Development,* September 2014, Vol. 51, No. 3

May, R. 1953. *Man's Search for Himself.* New York: W.W. Norton.

Nelsen, J. 1981. *Positive Discipline.* New York: Ballantine Books.

Ortiz-Ospina, E., and Roser, M. International Trade, https://ourworldindata.org/international-trade April 18, 2017.

Rogers, C. 1961. *On Becoming a Person.* Boston: Houghton Mifflin Company.

Rosenberg, M. 2003. *Nonviolent Communication: A Language of Life.* Encinitas, California: PuddleDancer Press.

Solter, A. 2018. Cooperative and Connected: Helping Children Flourish Without Punishments or Rewards. Goleta, CA: Shining Star Press.

Solter, A. 2001. The Aware Baby. Goleta, CA: Shining Star Press.

Solter, A. 1998: Tears and Tantrums: What to Do When Babies and Children Cry. Goleta, CA: Shining Star Press.

ABOUT THE AUTHOR

LAURA FOBLER was born in The Netherlands. After she received her master's degree in psychology, she started working as a consultant in a leading Dutch bank. While she worked with many clients, she discovered her true passion: interpersonal communication. She then decided to become a career coach. Working as such, she noticed how many people suffer from a lack of confidence, unable to name their true qualities. She realized that the vast majority have been brought up by well-intended parents who apparently don't know how confidence and self-esteem are nurtured, as so many people have self-esteem and confidence issues.

Laura, whose intention is always to help others, became a licensed PET instructor (Parent Effectiveness Training, also known as the Gordon Model). After conducting many parenting classes, she discovered that many parents are oblivious to the consequences of their own behavior toward their children, which often results in conflicts, both at home and globally. Realizing that the world is in turmoil, she is now dedicated to helping parents raise awareness of the connection between parenting style and conflicts. After doing extensive research, she came up with the Seven Simple Steps to World Peace.

www.ingramcontent.com/pod-product-compliance
Lightning Source LLC
Chambersburg PA
CBHW071735080526
44588CB00013B/2034